I0762725

Video Game Amigurumi

20+ Crochet Companions for Players and Fans

By Lee Sartori
With additional text by Kay Austin

INSIGHT EDITIONS
SAN RAFAEL • LOS ANGELES • LONDON

CONTENTS

7 **INTRODUCTION**

9 **Jonesy** - *Fortnite*

17 **Crewmate** - *Among Us*

21 **Korok** - *The Legend of Zelda*

27 **Chocobo** - *Final Fantasy*

33 **Blue Shell** - *Mario Kart*

39 **PAC-MAN and GHOSTS** - *PAC-MAN*

45 **Ryu** - *Street Fighter*

53 **Isabelle** - *Animal Crossing*

59 **Bag of Bells** - *Animal Crossing*

63 **Kirby** - *Kirby's Dream Land*

69 **Freddy** - *Five Nights at Freddy's*

77 **Pikmin** - *Pikmin*

83 **Murloc** - *World of Warcraft*

89 **Blue Chicken** - *Stardew Valley*

93 **Geralt** - *The Witcher*

101 **Sans** - *Undertale*

107 **Huggy Wuggy** - *Poppy Playtime*

113 **Sub-Zero** - *Mortal Kombat*

121 **Mr. Saturn** - *EarthBound*

125 **Zombie** - *Plants vs. Zombies*

133 **Mama** - *Cooking Mama*

PROJECT SKILL LEVELS

★ Beginner

★★ Intermediate

★★★ Advanced

INTRODUCTION

Video games have become a common comfort for gamers of all ages, whether that be in navigating the mazes of *PAC-MAN*, enjoying the comforts of an island getaway in *Animal Crossing: New Horizons*, or running across the fantastical landscapes of the *Final Fantasy* series. For many people, video games have left a strong impression on them, lingering in their minds years after a game has been set aside. Fans of *Mortal Kombat* can still hear the words "Finish him!" ringing in their ears, and anyone who's played *Mario Kart* knows the dread of seeing a Blue Shell circling overhead while in first place.

The amigurumi found in this book are sure to leave you with the same warm, fuzzy feelings as the characters and games from which they are drawn. The crewmate from *Among Us* is bound to bring to mind all of the game's "whodunit" hijinks, while the cuddly chocobo from *Final Fantasy* will serve as a reminder of your many adventures. Will Sans from *Undertale* make you cry, laugh, or shudder in fear of his fight?

As you stitch your way through these amigurumi, take care to remember the fond times you've had with these games—and maybe take note of any new faces you might want to meet! Perhaps making your own Korok will make you want to jump into *The Legend of Zelda: Breath of the Wild* or *The Legend of Zelda: Tears of the Kingdom* to find all of them hidden there. Or maybe the unique blue chicken from *Stardew Valley* will draw you into the chill, comforting life on the farm.

Whether you're a seasoned crochet artist or just starting out on your journey, you're sure to find a pattern in this book that suits your skill level, and with such a wide range of genres to be found, there's no doubt you'll find a character, critter, or item you recognize. Just remember: No matter how hard it gets, the point of a game is to have fun—and the same goes for crochet!

JONESY

SKILL LEVEL: ⭐⭐⭐

Formerly a high-ranking member of the Imagined Order, John "Jonesy" Jones of the popular battle royale game *Fortnite* was granted safety for his family and immortality for himself in exchange for his work. However, he came to realize the true curse of his immortality and defected. He and his snapshots worked alongside the Looper to instead bring down The Order and put a stop to their dangerous meddling with the Zero Point.

FINISHED MEASUREMENTS

Height: 9 in. / 22.86 cm

Width: 13 in. / 33.02 cm

YARN

Worsted weight (#4 medium) yarn, shown in Lion Brand Yarn *Heartland* (100% acrylic, 251 yd. / 230 m per 5 oz. / 142 g skein).

Color A: #126 Sequoia, 1 skein

Worsted weight (#4 medium) yarn, shown in Lion Brand Yarn *Basic Stitch Anti Pilling* (100% acrylic, 185 yd. / 170 m per 3.5 oz. / 100 g skein).

Color B: #184S Peachy, 1 skein

Color D: #125AA Truffle, 1 skein

Color H: #133A Pumpkin, 1 skein

Color F: #153 Black, 1 skein

Worsted weight (#4 medium) yarn, shown in Furls Crochet *Wander* (100% acrylic, 120 yd. / 109 m per 3.5 oz. / 100 g skein).

Color C: Foundry, 1 skein

Color G: Sprout, 1 skein

Worsted weight (#4 medium) yarn, shown in Lion Brand Yarn *Vanna's Choice* (100% acrylic, 170 yd. / 156 m per 3.5 oz. / 100 g skein).

Color E: #158I Mustard, 1 skein

HOOK

US G/6 (4 mm) crochet hook

NOTIONS

Polyester stuffing

Plastic mesh

Locking stitch markers

Tapestry needle

Pair of 6 mm black safety eyes

GAUGE

Gauge is not critical for this project. Ensure your stitches are tight so the stuffing won't show through.

SPECIAL STITCHES

Fpsc (front post single crochet): Insert hook from front to back around post of indicated stitch, yo and draw up a loop, yo and draw through 2 loops.

Invdec (invisible single crochet decrease): Insert hook in front loop only of each of next 2 sts, yarn over and draw through both sts, yarn over and draw through 2 loops on hook – 1 st decreased.

Popcorn (popcorn stitch): Work 5 dc in next st, drop loop on hook, insert hook from front to back in 1st dc of 5, place dropped loop on hook and draw it through the back of the 1st dc.

NOTES

Work in continuous rounds unless otherwise indicated.

ARMS (MAKE 2)

With **A**, make a magic ring.

Rnd 1: 6 sc in ring – 6 sc.

Rnd 2: 2 sc in each st around – 12 sc.

Rnds 3–4: Sc around.

Rnd 5: Popcorn, sc 11 – 12 sts.

Rnds 6–7: Sc around.

Rnd 8: Working in FLO, 2 sc in each st around, join to 1st sc with a sl st – 24 sc.

Rnd 9: Ch 1, in BLO of Rnd 8 sts, sc around, join to 1st sc with a sl st – 12 sc.

Change to **B**.

Rnd 10: Ch 1, in BLO sc around, join – 12 sc.

Rnd 11: Ch 1, 2 sc in 1st st, sc around, join – 13 sc.

Change to **C**.

Rnd 12: Ch 1 tightly, sc around, *do not join* – 13 sc.

Rnd 13: 2 sc in 1st st, sc around – 14 sc.

Rnd 14: Sc around.

Rnd 15: 2 sc in 1st st, sc around – 15 sc.

Rnds 16–18: Sc around.

Stuff Arms, then set aside to join to Body.

BOOT SOLES (MAKE 4)

With **A**.

Rnd 1: Ch 5, sc in 2nd ch from hook, sc 2, 3 sc in last, rotate to work on underside of ch, sc 3, 3 sc in last – 12 sc.

Rnd 2: *Sc 3, [2 sc in next st] x 3; rep from * around – 18 sc.

Rnd 3: *Sc 3, [2 sc, sc in next] x 3; rep from * around – 24 sc.

Fasten off 1st piece, but do not fasten off 2nd piece. Trace Boot Sole on a piece of plastic mesh. Cut out the shape and place mesh between 2 Boot Soles and continue to joining rnd.

Rnd 4 (joining): Working in BLO through both thicknesses, with plastic mesh sandwiched in between, sc around – 24 sc.

Fasten off. Continue to Boots.

BOOTS (MAKE 2)

With **C**.

Join to back of heel of Boot Sole.

Rnds 1–2: Ch 1, sc around, join – 24 sc.

Rnd 3: Ch 1, sc 8, [invdec, sc] x 3, sc 7, join – 21 sc.

Rnd 4: Ch 1, sc 8, [invdec] x 3, sc 7, join – 18 sc.

Rnds 5–8: Sc around.

Rnd 9: Ch 1, sc 8, working in BLO sc 6, sc 4 – 18 sc.

Rnd 10: Ch 1, working in FLO sl st 6, tr in next 6 FLO sts left from Rnd 9, working in FLO sl st 4 – 18 sts.

Fasten off.

LEGS (MAKE 2)

With **D**.

Join to center back of heel in BLO sts left from Rnd 10 of Boot.

Rnd 1: Ch 1, in BLO sc around, join – 18 sc.

Rnd 2: Ch 1 tightly, sc around, *do not join* – 18 sc.

Rnds 3–12: Sc around.

Fasten off 1st Leg, but do not fasten off 2nd Leg.

Rnd 13 (joining): Sc around, sl st in same st as 1st sc (sl st not counted as a st), sc in middle of inner thigh of 2nd Leg, sc around – 36 sc.

Rnds 14–21: Sc around.

Fasten off.

BOOT STRAPS (MAKE 5)

With **A** and leaving a long tail at start for sewing.

Row 1: Ch 18.

Fasten off, leaving a long tail for sewing. Using photo as a guide, secure a Strap around each ankle and around each Boot top below the tr sts. Set 5th Strap aside for Holster. Weave in ends.

HOLSTER

With **A**.

Rnd 1: Ch 5, sc in 2nd ch from hook, sc 2, 2 sc in last, rotate to work on underside of starting ch, sc 3, 2 sc in last – 10 sc.

Rnd 2: Working in BLO, sc around.

Rnds 3–4: Sc around.

Row 5: Sl st in next st, ch 1, sc 5, turn – 5 sc.

Rows 6–7: Ch 1, sc 5, turn – 5 sc.

Fasten off. Weave in ends.

HOLSTER STRAP

With **A** and leaving a long tail for sewing at start.

Row 1: Ch 36.

Fasten off, leaving a long tail for sewing. Using photo as a guide, secure Holster Strap around hip. Using 5th Boot Strap, secure it to upper Leg. Sew Holster to upper Leg. Weave in ends.

BODY

With **C**, join to center back of Leg.

Rnd 1: In BLO, sc around – 36 sc.

Rnd 2: [2 sc, sc 11] x 3 – 39 sc.

Rnd 3: [Sc 6, 2 sc in next, sc 6] x 3 – 42 sc.

Rnd 4: [2 sc, sc 13] x 3 – 45 sc.

Rnd 5: [Sc 7, 2 sc in next, sc 7] x 3 – 48 sc.

Rnd 6: [2 sc, sc 15] x 3 – 51 sc.

Rnd 7: [Sc 8, 2 sc in next, sc 8] x 3 – 54 sc.

Using 2 locking stitch markers, mark sides of Body for Arms, ensuring there are 24 sts for front of Body and 24 sts for back of Body between markers.

Rnd 8: Sc to 1st marker, sc in marker, holding Arm join by sc 15 around Arm ensuring thumb is facing Body, sc to 2nd marked st, sc in marked st, holding 2nd Arm in line with Body and with thumb facing Body, sc 15 around Arm to join, sc in remaining sts around – 84 sc.

Rnds 9–11: Sc around.

Rnd 12: [Sc 6, invdec, sc 6] around – 78 sc.

Rnd 13: [Invdec, sc 11] around – 72 sc.

Rnd 14: [Sc 5, invdec, sc 5] around – 66 sc.

Rnd 15: [Invdec, sc 9] around – 60 sc.

Rnd 16: [Sc 4, invdec, sc 4] around – 54 sc.

Rnd 17: [Invdec, sc 7] around – 48 sc.

Rnd 18: [Sc 3, invdec, sc 3] around – 42 sc.

Rnd 19: [Invdec, sc 5] around – 36 sc.

Rnd 20: [Sc 2, invdec, sc 2] around – 30 sc.

Fasten off. Stuff Body firmly, paying attention to stuffing shoulders. Continue to Head.

HEAD

With **B**.

Rnd 1: In BLO, sc around, join – 30 sc.

Rnd 2: Ch 1 tightly, [sc 4, invdec, sc 4] around, *do not join* – 27 sc.

Rnd 3: [Invdec, sc 7] around – 24 sc.

Rnd 4: Sc around.

Rnd 5: [2 sc, sc] around – 36 sc.

Rnd 6: Fpsc around – 36 sc.

Rnds 7–19: Sc around.

Add safety eyes between Rnds 14–15 approximately 8 sts apart. Using **B**, add nose over 3 sts between Rnds 11–12. Using **E**, add eyebrows over eyes. Using a strand of **B**, sew a stitch beside each eye and pull gently to cinch eyes together slightly, tying a knot inside Head to secure. Stuff Head and continue stuffing as work progresses.

Rnd 20: [Sc 2, invdec, sc 2] around – 30 sc.

Rnd 21: [Invdec, sc 3] around – 24 sc.

Rnd 22: [Sc, invdec, sc] around – 18 sc.

Rnd 23: [Invdec, sc] around – 12 sc.

Rnd 24: Invdec around – 6 sc.

Fasten off, leaving a long tail for sewing. Sew remaining 6 sts closed. Weave in ends.

EARS (MAKE 2)

With **B**.

Rnd 1: Ch 2, 4 sc in 2nd ch from hook.

Fasten off, leaving a long tail for sewing. Sew Ears to sides of Head in line with nose.

HAIR

With **E**.

Rnd 1: Ch 2, 6 sc in 2nd ch from hook – 6 sc.

Rnd 2: 2 sc in each st around – 12 sc.

Rnd 3: [2 sc, sc in next] around – 18 sc.

Rnd 4: [Sc, 2 sc in next, sc] around – 24 sc.

Rnd 5: [2 sc, sc 3] around – 30 sc.

Rnd 6: [Sc 2, 2 sc in next, sc 2] around – 36 sc.

Rnds 7–10: Sc around.

Rnd 11: Sc 15, turn – 15 sc.

Rnd 12: Do not ch 1, skip 1st st, sc 12, sc2tog – 13 sc.

Rnd 13: Do not ch 1, skip 1st st, sc 10, sc2tog – 11 sc.

Rnd 14: Do not ch 1, skip 1st st, sc 8, sc2tog – 9 sc.

Fasten off, leaving a long tail for sewing. Sew Hair to top of Head, with short rows at base of neck. Weave in ends.

BANGS

With **E**, leave a long tail at start for sewing.

Row 1: [Ch 4, sl st in 2nd ch from hook, sc in next, dc in last] x 2, ch 4, sl st in 2nd ch from hook, sc in next 2 chs, ch 3, sl st in 2nd ch from hook, sc in last.

Fasten off, leaving a long tail for sewing. Sew Bangs to front of Hair using photo as a guide. Weave in ends.

KNEEPADS (MAKE 2)

With **F**.

Row 1: Ch 24, sc in 2nd ch from hook, sc 4, turn – 5 sc.

Rows 2–4: Ch 1, sc 5, turn.

Row 5: Ch 1, sc 5, ch 18.

Fasten off. Using starting and ending chs, secure around knee. Weave in ends.

BELT

With **F**.

Rnd 1: Ch 6, sl st to form a ring, ch 1, sc in each ch around – 6 sc.

Rnds 2–31: Sc around.

Fasten off, leaving a long tail for sewing. Sew Belt around waist. Weave in ends.

JACKET SLEEVES (MAKE 2)

With **G**.

Rnd 1: Ch 15, sl st to form a ring, ch 1, sc in each ch around – 15 sc.

Rnds 2–8: Sc around.

Fasten off. Set Sleeves aside to join to Jacket.

JACKET

With **G** and leaving a long tail at start for sewing.

Row 1: Ch 37, 2 sc in 2nd ch from hook, sc 11, [2 sc, sc 11] x 2, turn – 39 sc.

Row 2: Ch 1, [sc 6, 2 sc, sc 6] across, turn – 42 sc.

Row 3: Ch 1, [2 sc, sc 13] across, turn – 45 sc.

Row 4: Ch 1, [sc 7, 2 sc, sc 7] across, turn – 48 sc.

Row 5: Ch 1, [2 sc, sc 15] across, turn – 51 sc.

Row 6: Ch 1, [sc 8, 2 sc, sc 8] across, turn – 54 sc.

Row 7: Ch 1, sc 14, holding Sleeve in line with sts sc 15 around Sleeve, sc 26, holding 2nd Sleeve in line with sts sc 15 around 2nd Sleeve, sc 14, turn – 84 sc.

Rows 8–10: Ch 1, sc across, turn.

Row 11: Ch 1, [sc 6, invdec, sc 6] across, turn – 78 sc.

Row 12: Ch 1, [invdec, sc 11] across, turn – 72 sc.

Row 13: Ch 1, [sc 5, invdec, sc 5] across, turn – 66 sc.

Row 14: Ch 1, [invdec, sc 9] across, turn – 60 sc.

Row 15: Ch 1, [sc 4, invdec, sc 4] across, turn – 54 sc.

Row 16: Ch 1, [invdec, sc 7] across, turn – 48 sc.

Row 17: Ch 1, [sc 3, invdec, sc 3] across, turn – 42 sc.

Fasten off, then weave in end. Place Jacket on Body. Using starting tail, sew 1st few rows of Jacket closed. Weave in end.

INNER JACKET COLLAR

With **H**.

Row 1: Ch 43, sc in 2nd ch from hook and in each ch across, turn – 42 sc.

Rows 2–3: Ch 1, sc across, turn.

Fasten off, then weave in ends. Set aside to join to Outer Jacket Collar.

OUTER JACKET COLLAR

With **G**.

Rows 1–3: Rep as per Inner Jacket Collar.

Row 4 (joining): Ch 1, holding Inner and Outer Jacket Collars together sc through both thicknesses around piece, placing 2 sc in each corner.

Fasten off, leaving a long tail for sewing. Sew Collar to top edge of Jacket. Weave in ends.

CROSSBODY STRAP

With **A**.

Row 1: Ch 50, sl st to form a ring, ch 1, sc in each ch around, join – 50 sc.

Fasten off, weave in ends. Add Strap around torso using photo as a guide.

CREWMATE

SKILL LEVEL: 

The life of an *Among Us* crewmate is a difficult one—in this party game, the crewmates need to complete a number of tasks to keep their ship or station up and running, all while dodging the deadly imposters hiding among them, attempting to sabotage them at every turn. Despite the danger to their lives, they can't stop. They need to make sure the course is correct, the wiring is functional, and the vents are clean—wait a second . . .

FINISHED MEASUREMENTS

Height: 5 in. / 12.7 cm

Width: 4 in. / 10.16 cm

YARN

Worsted weight (#4 medium) yarn, shown in Furls Crochet *Wander* (100% acrylic, 120 yd. / 109 m per 3.5 oz. / 100 g skein).

Color A: Pomegranate, 1 skein

Color B: Mist, 1 skein

Color C: Obsidian, 1 skein

HOOK

US G/6 (4 mm) crochet hook

NOTIONS

Plastic mesh, small piece

Polyester stuffing

Stitch markers

Tapestry needle

White felt, small amount

SPECIAL STITCHES

Invdec (invisible single crochet decrease): Insert hook in front loop only of each of next 2 sts, yarn over and draw through both sts, yarn over and draw through 2 loops on hook – 1 st decreased.

NOTES

Work in continuous rounds unless otherwise indicated.

FEET BOTTOMS (MAKE 4)

With **A**.

Rnd 1: Ch 2, 6 sc in 2nd ch from hook – 6 sc.

Rnd 2: 2 sc in each st around – 12 sc.

Rnd 3: [2 sc in next, sc in next] around – 18 sc.

Fasten off 1st Foot Bottom, but do not fasten off 2nd piece. Trace Foot Bottom on a piece of plastic mesh. Cut out the shape and place mesh between 2 Feet Bottoms and continue to joining rnd.

Rnd 4 (joining): Working in BLO, sc around through both thicknesses with plastic mesh in between.

Continue to Legs.

LEGS (MAKE 2)

With **A**.

Rnds 1–5: Sc around.

Fasten off 1st Leg, but do not fasten off 2nd Leg.

Rnd 6: Ch 3, sc in 1st Leg, sc in next 17 sts, sc 3 across ch-3, sc 18 around 2nd Leg, sc in underside of ch-3 – 42 sc.

Stuff Legs. Continue to Body.

BODY

With **A**.

Mark 1st st of this rnd as new start of rnd. Move marker as work progresses.

Rnds 1–3: Sc around.

Rnd 4: [2 sc, sc 6] around – 48 sc.

Rnds 5–20: Sc around.

Rnd 21: [Sc 3, invdec, sc 3] around – 42 sc.

Rnd 22: [Invdec, sc 5] around – 36 sc.

Rnd 23: [Sc 2, invdec, sc 2] around – 30 sc.

Stuff Body firmly. Continue stuffing as work progresses.

Rnd 24: [Invdec, sc 3] around – 24 sc.

Rnd 25: [Sc, invdec, sc] around – 18 sc.

Rnd 26: [Invdec, sc] around – 12 sc.

Rnd 27: Invdec around – 6 sc.

Fasten off, leaving a long tail for sewing. Sew remaining 6 sts closed.

BACKPACK

With **A**.

Row 1: Ch 13, sc in 2nd ch from hook and in each ch across, turn – 12 sc.

Rows 2–12: Ch 1, sc across, turn.

Using plastic mesh, trace Rows 1–12 and cut out square. Set aside.

Row 13: Ch 1, working in BLO sc across, turn – 12 sc.

Rows 14–16: Ch 1, sc across, turn.

Row 17: Rep Row 13.

Rows 18–28: Ch 1, sc across, turn.

Row 29: Rep Row 13.

Rows 30–32: Ch 1, sc across, turn.

Fasten off, leaving a long tail for sewing. Sew Row 1 to Row 32 in BLO. Insert plastic mesh square. Stuff lightly. Continue to Backpack Sides.

BACKPACK SIDES (MAKE 2)

With **A**.

Row 1: Ch 5, sc in 2nd ch from hook and in each ch across, turn – 4 sc.

Rows 2–12: Ch 1, sc across, turn.

Fasten off, leaving a long tail for sewing. Sew Backpack Sides to each side of Backpack. Weave in ends. Sew Backpack to back of Body.

VISOR

With **B**.

Rnd 1: Ch 9, sc in 2nd ch from hook, sc in next 6 chs, 3 sc in last, rotate to work on underside of ch, sc 7, 3 sc in last ch – 20 sc.

Rnd 2: [Sc 7, 2 sc in next 3 sts] x 2 – 26 sc.

Rnds 3–4: Sc around.

Change to **C**.

Rnd 5: Working in FLO, sc around, join.

Rnd 6: Ch 1, working in BLO sc around, join.

Fasten off, leaving a long tail for sewing. Stuff Visor lightly. Sew Visor to front of Body between Rnds 11–19.

FINISHING

Cut a small oval out of the white felt and add to top right corner of Visor.

KOROK

SKILL LEVEL: ⭐⭐

"Yahaha! You've found them!" Introduced in *The Legend of Zelda: The Wind Waker* and making a return in *Breath of the Wild* and *Tears of the Kingdom*, Koroks come in many shapes and sizes, always wearing a leaflike mask. Though many can be found living in their forest home, they're also quite curious and fond of traveling to all corners of Hyrule—despite the potentially harsh or dangerous environments in which they might find themselves.

FINISHED MEASUREMENTS

Height: 6 in. / 15.24 cm

Width: 5 in. / 12.7 cm

YARN

Worsted weight (#4 medium) yarn, shown in Furls Crochet *Wander* (100% acrylic, 120 yd. / 109 m per 3.5 oz. / 100 g skein).

Color A: Fawn, 1 skein

Worsted weight (#4 medium) yarn, shown in Loops & Threads *Impeccable* (100% acrylic, 285 yd. / 260 m per 4.5 oz. / 127 g skein).

Color B: #01010 Heather, 1 skein

Worsted weight (#4 medium) yarn, shown in Lion Brand Yarn *Vanna's Choice* (100% acrylic, 170 yd. / 156 m per 3.5 oz. / 100 g skein).

Color C: #860-172C Kelly Green, 1 skein

HOOK

US G/6 (4 mm) crochet hook

NOTIONS

Stitch markers

Tapestry needle

Polyester stuffing

Black embroidery thread, small amount

One 9 mm black safety eye

One 6 mm black safety eye

GAUGE

Gauge is not critical for this project. Ensure your stitches are tight so the stuffing won't show through.

SPECIAL STITCHES

Invdec (invisible single crochet decrease): Insert hook in front loop only of each of next 2 sts, yarn over and draw through both sts, yarn over and draw through 2 loops on hook – 1 st decreased.

NOTES

Work in continuous rounds unless otherwise indicated.

FEET (MAKE 2)

With **A**.

Rnd 1: Ch 2, 4 sc in 2nd ch from hook – 4 sc.

Rnd 2: Working in BLO, 2 sc in 1st st, sc 3 – 5 sc.

Change to **B**.

Rnd 3: 2 sc, sc 4 – 6 sc.

Rnd 4: Sc around.

Fasten off 1st Foot, but do not fasten off 2nd piece. Continue to Body.

BODY

Rnd 1: Ch 9, sc in 1st Foot to join Feet together, sc in next 5 sts, sc in each ch of ch-9, sc 6 around 2nd Foot – 21 sc.

Change to **A**.

Rnd 2: Sc in underside of next 9 chs, sc around – 30 sc.

Rnd 3: [Sc 2, 2 sc, sc 2] around – 36 sc.

Begin colorwork with **A** and **B**, carrying unused color beneath sts as work progresses.

Rnd 4: [Sc 2 **B**, sc 16 **A**] x 2 – 36 sc

Rnd 5: [Sc 4 **B**, sc 14 **A**] x 2.

Rnd 6: With **B** only [2 sc, sc 5] around – 42 sc.

Rnd 7: With **B** only, sc around.

Rnd 8: [Sc 2 **A**, sc 19 **B**] x 2.

Rnd 9: [Sc 4 **A**, sc 17 **B**] x 2.

Rnd 10: [Sc 12 **A**, sc 9 **B**] x 2.

Rnd 11: With **A** only [invdec, sc 5] around – 36 sc.

Rnd 12: With **A** only [sc 2, invdec, sc 2] around – 30 sc.

Rnd 13: With **A** only [invdec, sc 3] around – 24 sc.

Rnd 14: [Sc 3 **B**, sc 3 **A**] x 4.

Rnd 15: With **A** only, sc 9, skip next 9 sts, sc 6 – 15 sc.

Begin working Spike. Skipped sts will be worked for a 2nd Spike further in pattern.

Rnd 16: With **A**, invdec, sc 3, with **B** [invdec, sc 3] x 2 – 12 sc.

Rnd 17: With **A** sc, invdec, sc, with **B** [sc, invdec, sc] x 2 – 9 sc.

Rnd 18: With **A** sc, invdec, with **B** [sc, invdec] x 2 – 6 sc.

Rnd 19: With **B** only, invdec around – 3 sc.

Stuff Legs, Body, and Spike through hole made in Rnd 15. Continue to Spike.

SPIKE

Leaving a long tail at start for sewing, join **B** to any skipped st of Rnd 15 to work 2nd Spike.

Rnds 1–3: Sc around – 9 sc.

Change to **A**.

Rnd 4: [Invdec, sc] x 3 – 6 sc.

Rnds 5–6: Sc around.

Change to **B**.

Rnd 7: Invdec around – 3 sc.

Stuff Spike. Fasten off, leaving a long tail for sewing. Sew remaining 3 sts closed. Using starting tail, sew gap between Spikes closed. Weave in ends.

ARMS (MAKE 2)

With **A** and leaving a long tail at start for sewing.

Rnd 1: Ch 6, join with a sl st to form a ring, 6 sc in ring – 6 sc.

Rnd 2: Sc around.

Rnd 3: Invdec, sc 4 – 5 sc.

Rnd 4: Invdec, sc 3 – 4 sc.

Rnd 5: Invdec, sc 2 – 3 sc.

Fasten off, leaving a long tail for sewing. Sew remaining 3 sts closed. Using starting tail, sew Arms to Body between Rnds 9–11. Weave in ends.

LEAF

With **C**.

Row 1: Ch 2, sc in 2nd ch from hook, turn – 1 sc.

Row 2: Ch 1, 3 sc in 1st st, turn – 3 sc.

Row 3: Ch 1, 2 sc, sc across to last, 2 sc in last, turn – 5 sc.

Rows 4–5: Rep Row 3 – 9 sc at end of Row 5.

Row 6: Ch 1, sc, hdc, (dc, tr, dc) in next, hdc, working in next st (sc, ch 4, sc in 2nd ch from hook, sc in next 2 ch, sc), hdc, (dc, tr, dc) in next, hdc, sc in last – 17 sts.

Fasten off, leaving a long tail for sewing. Add safety eyes to Leaf using photo as a guide. Using black embroidery thread, add mouth detail and small line under small eye. Sew Leaf to front of Body. Weave in ends.

CHOCOBO

SKILL LEVEL: ★★

These beloved yellow birds are the stalwart steeds found across the *Final Fantasy* franchise. They've made an appearance in every mainline game from *Final Fantasy II* onward, as well as in many spin-off games—including some where one of these charming companions serves as the protagonist. From the streets of Lostime to the lands of Valisthea, there's no doubt about it—these feathered friends are the perfect companion for any *kweh*-st!

FINISHED MEASUREMENTS

Height: 9 in. / 22.86 cm

Width: 6.5 in. / 16.51 cm

YARN

Worsted weight (#4 medium) yarn, shown in Lion Brand Yarn *Vanna's Choice* (100% acrylic, 170 yd. / 156 m per 3.5 oz. / 100 g skein).

Color A: #860-158I Mustard, 1 skein

Color B: #860-134A Terracotta, 1 skein

Color C: #860-100 White, 1 skein

HOOK

US G/6 (4 mm) crochet hook

NOTIONS

Stitch markers

White felt, small amount

One pair each of 24 mm black and blue safety eyes

Polyester stuffing

Tapestry needle

Black embroidery thread, small amount

GAUGE

Gauge is not critical for this project. Ensure your stitches are tight so the stuffing won't show through.

SPECIAL STITCHES

Invdec (invisible single crochet decrease): Insert hook in front loop only of each of next 2 sts, yarn over and draw through both sts, yarn over and draw through 2 loops on hook – 1 st decreased.

NOTES

Work in continuous rounds unless otherwise indicated.

HEAD

With **A**.

Rnd 1: Ch 2, 6 sc in 2nd ch from hook – 6 sc.

Rnd 2: 2 sc in each st around – 12 sc.

Rnd 3: [2 sc, sc in next] around – 18 sc.

Rnd 4: [Sc, 2 sc in next, sc] around – 24 sc.

Rnd 5: [2 sc, sc 3] around – 30 sc.

Rnd 6: [Sc 2, 2 sc in next, sc 2] around – 36 sc.

Rnd 7: [2 sc, sc 5] around – 42 sc.

Rnds 8–14: Sc around.

Rnd 15: [Invdec, sc 5] around – 36 sc.

Rnd 16: [Sc 2, invdec, sc 2] around – 30 sc.

Rnd 17: [Invdec, sc 3] around – 24 sc.

Rnd 18: [Sc, invdec, sc] around – 18 sc.

Add a ring of white felt behind each safety eye. Add safety eyes to Head between Rnds 7–12. Stuff. Continue stuffing as work progresses.

Rnd 19: Working in BLO [sc, 2 sc in next, sc] around – 24 sc.

Continue to Body.

BODY

Continuing with **A**, stuff as work progresses.

Rnd 1: [2 sc, sc 3] around – 30 sc.

Rnd 2: [Sc 2, 2 sc in next, sc 2] around – 36 sc.

Rnd 3: [2 sc, sc 5] around – 42 sc.

Rnds 4–10: Sc around.

Rnd 11: [Invdec, sc 5] around – 36 sc.

Rnd 12: [Sc 2, invdec, sc 2] around – 30 sc.

Rnd 13: [Invdec, sc 3] around – 24 sc.

Rnd 14: [Sc, invdec, sc] around – 18 sc.

Rnd 15: [Invdec, sc] around – 12 sc.

Rnd 16: Invdec around – 6 sc.

Fasten off, leaving a long tail for sewing. Sew remaining 6 sts closed. Weave in ends.

LARGE SPIKES (MAKE 3)

With **A**.

Rnd 1: Ch 2, 4 sc in 2nd ch from hook – 4 sc.

Rnd 2: [2 sc, sc in next] around – 6 sc.

Rnd 3: [2 sc, sc 2] around – 8 sc.

Rnd 4: [2 sc, sc 3] around – 10 sc.

Rnd 5: [2 sc, sc 4] around – 12 sc.

Rnd 6: [2 sc, sc 5] around – 14 sc.

Rnd 7: Sc around.

Rnd 8: [Invdec, sc 5] around – 12 sc.

Rnd 9: [Invdec, sc 4] around – 10 sc.

Fasten off, leaving a long tail for sewing. Stuff the Large Spikes. Sew 1 Large Spike between Rnds 3–7 of middle of back of Head using photo as a guide. Between Rnds 6–10, sew 1 Large Spike on either side of the middle Large Spike, approximately 3 sts away from the middle Large Spike on either side of Head. Weave in ends.

SMALL SPIKES (MAKE 3)

With **A**.

Rnd 1: Ch 2, 3 sc in 2nd ch from hook – 3 sc.

Rnd 2: 2 sc, sc 2 – 4 sc.

Rnd 3: 2 sc, sc 3 – 5 sc.

Fasten off, leaving a long tail for sewing. Sew 2 Small Spikes to the sides of Head between Rnds 12–15. Sew remaining Spike to center of forehead using photo as a guide. Weave in ends.

TAIL FEATHERS (MAKE 5)

With **A**.

Rnd 1: Ch 2, 4 sc in 2nd ch from hook – 4 sc.

Rnd 2: [2 sc, sc in next] around – 6 sc.

Rnd 3: [2 sc, sc 2] around – 8 sc.

Rnd 4: [2 sc, sc 3] around – 10 sc.

Rnd 5: [2 sc, sc 4] around – 12 sc.

Rnd 6: [2 sc, sc 5] around – 14 sc.

Rnds 7–11: Sc around.

Rnd 12: [Invdec, sc 5] around – 12 sc.

Rnd 13: [Invdec, sc 4] around – 10 sc.

Fasten off, leaving a long tail for sewing. Stuff. Sew Tail Feathers to back of Body. Weave in ends.

WING TIPS (MAKE 6)

With **A**.

Rnd 1: Ch 2, 3 sc in 2nd ch from hook – 3 sc.

Rnd 2: 2 sc, sc 2 – 4 sc.

Rnd 3: 2 sc, sc 3 – 5 sc.

Rnd 4: 2 sc, sc 4 – 6 sc.

Fasten off.

WINGS (MAKE 2)

With 3 Wing Tips, join A to 1st piece. Rnd 1 will be joining 3 Wing Tips together.

Rnd 1: Sc 3 on 1st Wing Tip, sc 3 on 2nd Wing Tip, sc 6 around 3rd Wing Tip, rotate to work on back of joined pieces, sc 3 on center Wing Tip, sc 3 on beginning Wing Tip – 18 sc.

Rnds 2–7: Sc around.

Rnd 8: [Invdec, sc] around – 12 sc.

Stuff Wing lightly.

Rnd 9: Invdec around – 6 sc.

Fasten off, leaving a long tail for sewing. Sew remaining 6 sts closed. Sew assembled Wings to sides of Body. Weave in ends.

BEAK

With **B**.

Rnd 1: Ch 2, 3 sc in 2nd ch from hook – 3 sc.

Rnd 2: 2 sc, sc 2 – 4 sc.

Rnd 3: 2 sc, sc 3 – 5 sc.

Rnd 4: 2 sc, sc 4 – 6 sc.

Rnd 5: 2 sc in each st around – 12 sc.

Rnd 6: [2 sc, sc] around – 18 sc.

Fasten off, leaving a long tail for sewing. Stuff lightly. Sew Beak to Head, between eyes.

CLAWS (MAKE 4)

With **C**.

Rnd 1: Ch 2, 4 sc in 2nd ch from hook – 4 sc.

Rnd 2: [2 sc, sc in next] around – 6 sc.

Rnd 3: Sc around.

Fasten off, then continue to Foot.

FEET (MAKE 2)

With **B**. With 2 Claws, join to 1st piece. Rnd 1 will be joining 2 Claws together.

Rnd 1: Sc 6 on 1st Claw, sc 6 on 2nd Claw to join – 12 sc.

Rnds 2–5: Sc around.

Rnd 6: Ch 3, skip 3 sc (*leg hole made*), sc 9 – 9 sc.

Rnd 7: Sc in each ch and sc around – 12 sc.

Rnd 8: Invdec around – 6 sc.

Rnd 9: Sc around.

Fasten off, leaving a long tail for sewing. Sew remaining 6 sts closed. Stuff Foot through leg hole. Continue to Legs.

LEGS (MAKE 2)

With **B**, join to 1st skipped st of Rnd 6 of Foot.

Rnd 1: Ch 1, sc in 3 sc, sc in gap before underside of ch-3, sc in underside of next 3 chs, sc in gap before starting sc – 8 sc.

Rnds 2–8: Sc around.

Fasten off, leaving a long tail for sewing. Stuff Leg. Sew Leg to bottom of Body.

BLUE SHELL

SKILL LEVEL: 

A familiar sight across the various *Mario Kart* games, the Blue Shell—formerly known as a Spiny Shell—has ruined more than a few days. A Green Shell can be dodged, a Red Shell can be blocked with a Banana Peel, but the Blue Shell always, with very few exceptions, seeks out the first-place racer. While it's only a rare item, even for those in last place, it's a frequent-enough occurrence that everyone knows what's about to happen when it starts to circle. This Blue Shell, however, is 100 percent safe to hold on to while you make your friends eat your dust.

FINISHED MEASUREMENTS

Height: 4 in. / 10.16 cm

Width: 4 in. / 10.16 cm

YARN

Worsted weight (#4 medium) yarn, shown in Furls Crochet *Wander* (100% acrylic, 120 yd. / 109 m per 3.5 oz. / 100 g skein).

Color A: Caspian, 1 skein

Color B: Alabaster, 1 skein

Color D: Obsidian, 1 skein

Worsted weight (#4 medium) yarn, shown in Loops & Threads *Impeccable* (100% acrylic, 285 yd. / 260 m per 4.5 oz. / 127 g skein).

Color C: #01010 Heather, 1 skein

HOOK

US G/6 (4 mm) crochet hook

NOTIONS

Stitch markers

Tapestry needle

Polyester stuffing

Black embroidery thread, small amount

GAUGE

Gauge is not critical for this project. Ensure your stitches are tight so the stuffing won't show through.

SPECIAL STITCHES

Invdec (invisible single crochet decrease): Insert hook in front loop only of each of next 2 sts, yarn over and draw through both sts, yarn over and draw through 2 loops on hook – 1 st decreased.

NOTES

Work in continuous rounds unless otherwise indicated.

TOP SHELL

With **A**.

Rnd 1: Ch 2, 6 sc in 2nd ch from hook – 6 sc.

Rnd 2: 2 sc in each st around – 12 sc.

Rnd 3: [2 sc, sc in next] around – 18 sc.

Rnd 4: [Sc, 2 sc in next, sc] around – 24 sc.

Rnd 5: [2 sc, sc 3] around – 30 sc.

Rnd 6: [Sc 2, 2 sc in next, sc 2] around – 36 sc.

Rnd 7: [2 sc, sc 5] around – 42 sc.

Rnd 8: [Sc 3, 2 sc in next, sc 3] around – 48 sc.

Rnd 9: [2 sc, sc 7] around – 54 sc.

Rnds 10–13: Sc around.

Fasten off, leaving a long tail for sewing. Using **D**, embroider a hexagon between Rnds 1–5 of Top Shell. Between Rnds 6–12, embroider 6 adjoining hexagons off center hexagon. There will be 7 hexagons total embroidered on Top Shell.

SPIKES (MAKE 7)

With **B**.

Rnd 1: Ch 2, 4 sc in 2nd ch from hook – 4 sc.

Rnd 2: [2 sc, sc in next] around – 6 sc.

Rnd 3: [2 sc, sc 2] around – 8 sc.

Rnd 4: [2 sc, sc 3] around – 10 sc.

Rnd 5: [2 sc, sc 4] around – 12 sc.

Fasten off, leaving a long tail for sewing. Stuff Spikes lightly. Sew 1 Spike in the center of each of the 7 hexagons embroidered on Top Shell.

BOTTOM SHELL

With **C**.

Rnds 1–13: Rep Rnds 1–13 of Top Shell.

Fasten off, leaving a long tail for sewing. Seam Top Shell and Bottom Shell together through BLO to leave a sewing edge for the Shell Edge. Stuff Shell lightly as work progresses.

SHELL EDGE

With **B**.

Rnd 1: Ch 4, join with a sl st to form a ring, ch 1, 6 sc in ring – 6 sc.

Remaining Rnds: Sc around, creating a long tube. Continue until the tube wraps around the middle of the Shell where the two Shells meet. Fasten off, leaving a long tail for sewing. Sew ends together and secure Shell Edge to center of Shell. Weave in ends.

LEG HOLES (MAKE 4)

With **D**, make a magic ring.

Rnd 1: 3 sc in ring, ch 1 to fasten off – 3 sc.

Leave a long tail for sewing. Sew Leg Holes in line with 4 side Spikes under Shell Edge.

HEAD HOLE

With **D**.

Rnd 1: Ch 2, 3 sc in 2nd ch from hook, turn – 3 sc.

Rnd 2: Ch 1, 2 sc in each st across – 6 sc.

Fasten off, leaving a long tail for sewing. Sew Head Hole in line with front Spike under Shell Edge.

NECK LINING

With **C**.

Rnd 1: Ch 4, sl st to form a ring, 4 sc in ring – 4 sc.

Rnds 2–9: Sc around.

Fasten off, leaving a long tail for sewing. Sew Neck Lining around Head Hole. Weave in ends.

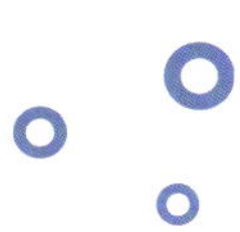

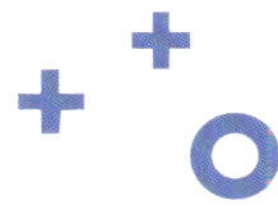

PAC-MAN AND GHOSTS

SKILL LEVEL: ☆

Originally released in 1980, *PAC-MAN* was intended to be a game that, compared to other games made during that time, relied less on violence. Instead, it's a game of chase. First the player guides PAC-MAN through a maze of PAC-DOTS, forever pursued by the four GHOSTS: BLINKY, PINKY, INKY, and CLYDE. Then, once PAC-MAN eats a POWER-PELLET, the chase reverses—PAC-MAN has a brief window to hunt down the GHOSTS for extra points before the cycle starts over again.

FINISHED MEASUREMENTS

Height: 3 in. / 7.62 cm

Width: 3 in. / 7.62 cm

YARN

Worsted weight (#4 medium) yarn, shown in WeCrochet *Brava Worsted* (100% acrylic, 218 yd. / 199 m per 3.5 oz. / 100 g skein).

Color A: Cornflower, 1 skein

Color B: Cotton Candy, 1 skein

Worsted weight (#4 medium) yarn, shown in Furls Crochet *Wander* (100% acrylic, 120 yd. / 109 m per 3.5 oz. / 100 g skein).

Color C: Pomegranate, 1 skein

Color D: Marmalade, 1 skein

DK weight (#3 light) yarn, shown in WeCrochet *Palette* (100% wool, 231 yd. / 211 m per 1.75 oz. / 50 g skein).

Color E: #23728 White, 1 skein

DK weight (#3 light) yarn, shown in Lion Brand Yarn *24/7 Cotton DK* (100% cotton, 273 yd. / 250 m per 3.5 oz. / 100 g skein).

Color F: #157AH Lemon Drop, 1 skein

HOOKS

US G/6 (4 mm) crochet hook

US 1.5 mm steel crochet hook

NOTIONS

Stitch markers

Polyester stuffing

Tapestry needle

Hole punch

Blue felt, small amount

Fabric glue

GAUGE

Gauge is not critical for this project. Ensure your stitches are tight so the stuffing won't show through.

NOTES

Work in continuous rounds unless otherwise indicated.

GHOSTS (MAKE 1 EACH IN A, B, C, AND D)

BODY

With larger hook and **A**, **B**, **C**, or **D**.

Rnd 1: Ch 2, 6 sc in 2nd ch from hook – 6 sc.

Rnd 2: 2 sc in each st around – 12 sc.

Rnd 3: [2 sc, sc in next] around – 18 sc.

Rnd 4: [Sc, 2 sc in next, sc] around – 24 sc.

Rnd 5: [2 sc, sc 3] around – 30 sc.

Rnd 6: [Sc 2, 2 sc in next, sc 2] around – 36 sc.

Rnds 7–14: Sc around.

Rnd 15: [Ch 6, skip 5 sc, sl st in next sc] around – 6 ch-6 spaces and 6 sl sts.

Continue to Spikes.

SPIKES (MAKE 6)

With larger hook and continuing in same color.

Rnd 1: Join to 1st skipped sc of Rnd 14 of Body, ch 1, sc in same st, sc in next 4 sc, sc in sl st, sc in next 6 chs, join to starting sc to form a rnd – 12 sc.

Rnd 2: [Sc 2, invdec] x 3 – 9 sc.

Rnd 3: [Sc, invdec] x 3 – 6 sc.

Fasten off, leaving a long tail for sewing. Sew remaining 6 sts closed. Weave in ends.

BOTTOM

With larger hook and continuing in same color.

Rnd 1: Ch 2, 6 sc in 2nd ch from hook – 6 sc.

Rnd 2: 2 sc in each st around – 12 sc.

Rnd 3: [2 sc, sc in next] around – 18 sc.

Rnd 4: [Sc, 2 sc in next, sc] around – 24 sc.

Rnd 5: [2 sc, sc in next 3] around – 30 sc.

Fasten off, leaving a long tail for sewing.

EYES (MAKE 2)

With smaller hook and **E**.

Rnd 1: Ch 2, 6 sc in 2nd ch from hook – 6 sc.

Rnd 2: 2 sc in each st around – 12 sc.

Rnd 3: [2 sc in next, sc] around – 18 sc.

Fasten off, leaving a long tail for sewing.

FINISHING

Sew Bottom to Spikes at underside of Body. Attach Eyes between Rnds 6–10 of Body, approximately 1 in. / 2.54 cm apart. Use a hole punch and blue felt to create irises for Eyes. Glue irises to Eyes using photos as a guide.

PAC-MAN

BODY

With larger hook and **F** held double stranded.

Rnd 1: Ch 2, 6 sc in 2nd ch from hook – 6 sc.

Rnd 2: 2 sc in each st around – 12 sc.

Rnd 3: [2 sc, sc in next] around – 18 sc.

Rnd 4: [Sc, 2 sc in next, sc] around – 24 sc.

Rnd 5: [2 sc, sc 3] around – 30 sc.

Rnd 6: [Sc 2, 2 sc in next, sc 2] around – 36 sc.

Rnds 7–8: Sc around.

Rnd 9: Ch 18, skip next 18 sts, sc 18 around – 18 sc.

Rnd 10: Sc in each ch and sc around – 36 sc.

Rnds 11–12: Sc around.

Rnd 13: [Sc 2, invdec, sc 2] around – 30 sc.

Rnd 14: [Invdec, sc 3] around – 24 sc.

Rnd 15: [Sc, invdec, sc] around – 18 sc.

Rnd 16: [Invdec, sc] around – 12 sc.

Rnd 17: Invdec around – 6 sc.

Fasten off, leaving a tail for sewing. Sew remaining 6 sts closed.

MOUTH

With larger hook and **F** held double stranded.

Rnd 1: Ch 2, 6 sc in 2nd ch from hook – 6 sc.

Rnd 2: 2 sc in each st around – 12 sc.

Rnd 3: [2 sc, sc in next] around – 18 sc.

Rnd 4: [Sc, 2 sc in next, sc] around – 24 sc.

Rnd 5: [2 sc, sc 3] around – 30 sc.

Rnd 6: [Sc 2, 2 sc in next, sc 2] around – 36 sc.

Fasten off, leaving a long tail for sewing.

FINISHING

Stuff PAC-MAN lightly. Sew Mouth insert to opening of Rnd 9 of Body, folding the piece in half at the back of the Mouth. Weave in ends.

RYU

SKILL LEVEL: ★★★

The well-known main protagonist of the *Street Fighter* series, Ryu has a constant presence in the franchise's media. Not only has he made an appearance in every *Street Fighter* game to date, but also in every official crossover the franchise has had. Though he seems distant due to his training often taking him away from the "modern world," Ryu is a kind-hearted warrior, ready to jump in and help those less fortunate.

FINISHED MEASUREMENTS

Height: 13 in. / 33.02 cm

Width: 8 in. / 20.32 cm

YARN

Worsted weight (#4 medium) yarn, shown in Lion Brand Yarn *Basic Stitch Anti Pilling* (100% acrylic, 185 yd. / 170 m per 3.5 oz. / 100 g skein).

Color A: #116H Beech, 1 skein

Color C: #100 White, 1 skein

Color D: #153 Black, 1 skein

Worsted weight (#4 medium) yarn, shown in Lion Brand Yarn *Vanna's Choice* (100% acrylic, 170 yd. / 156 m per 3.5 oz. / 100 g skein).

Color B: #113 Scarlet, 1 skein

HOOK

US G/6 (4 mm) crochet hook

NOTIONS

Stitch markers

Polyester stuffing

Tapestry needle

Plastic mesh, small piece

Pair of 6 mm black safety eyes

GAUGE

Gauge is not critical for this project. Ensure your stitches are tight so the stuffing won't show through.

SPECIAL STITCHES

Fpsc (front post single crochet): Insert hook from front to back around post of indicated stitch, yo and draw up a loop, yo and draw through 2 loops.

Invdec (invisible single crochet decrease): Insert hook in front loop only of each of next 2 sts, yarn over and draw through both sts, yarn over and draw through 2 loops on hook – 1 st decreased.

Popcorn (popcorn stitch): Work 5 dc in next st, drop loop on hook, insert hook from front to back in 1st dc of 5, place dropped loop on hook and draw it through the back of the 1st dc.

NOTES

Work in continuous rounds unless otherwise indicated.

ARMS (MAKE 2)

With **A**, make a magic ring.

Rnd 1: 6 sc in ring – 6 sc.

Rnd 2: 2 sc in each st around – 12 sc.

Change to **B**.

Rnd 3: Ch 1, working in BLO, sc around, join – 12 sc.

Rnd 4: Ch 1, sc around, join.

Rnd 5: Ch 1, with **A** Popcorn, with **B** sc 11 – 12 sts.

Continuing with **B**.

Rnds 6–7: Ch 1, sc around, join.

Stuff hand lightly.

Rnd 8: Ch 1, invdec around – 6 sc.

Rnd 9: Ch 1, [2 sc, sc] around, join – 9 sc.

Rnd 10: Ch 1, [2 sc, sc 2] around – 12 sc.

Fasten off **B**, then continue with **A**.

Rnd 11: Ch 1, working in BLO, 2 sc in 1st st, sc around, join – 13 sc.

Rnd 12: Ch 1 tightly, sc around, *do not join* – 13 sc.

Rnd 13: 2 sc, sc around – 14 sc.

Rnd 14: Sc around.

Rnd 15: 2 sc, sc around – 15 sc.

Rnds 16–18: Sc around.

Fasten off. Stuff Arms and set aside to join to Body.

FEET (MAKE 2)

With **A**, begin working Sole (make 4).

Rnd 1: Ch 5, sc in 2nd ch from hook, sc 2, 3 sc in last, rotate to work on underside of ch, sc 3, 3 sc in last – 12 sc.

Rnd 2: *Sc 3, [2 sc in next st] x 3; rep from * around – 18 sc.

Rnd 3: *Sc 3, [2 sc, sc in next] x 3; rep from * around – 24 sc.

Fasten off 1st piece, but do not fasten off 2nd piece. Trace Sole on a piece of plastic mesh. Cut out the shape and place mesh between 2 Soles and continue to joining rnd.

Rnd 4 (joining): Working in BLO through both thicknesses, with plastic mesh sandwiched in between, sc around – 24 sc.

Fasten off, then join to back of heel.

Rnds 5–6: Ch 1, sc around, join – 24 sc.

Rnd 7: Ch 1, sc 8, [invdec, sc] x 3, sc 7, join – 21 sc.

Rnd 8: Ch 1, sc 8, [invdec] x 3, sc 7, join – 18 sc.

Rnds 9–10: Sc around. Fasten off. Continue to Pant Legs.

PANT LEGS (MAKE 2)

With **C**, join to center back of heel.

Rnd 1: Ch 1, sc around, join, *turn* – 18 sc.

Rnd 2 (Ripped Cuff): *Ch 3, sl st in 2nd ch from hook, sc in next, skip next st of Rnd 1, in BLO sl st 2; rep from * around, *turn*.

Rnd 3: Working in FLO sts left from Rnd 2, sc around – 18 sc.

Rnds 4–12: Sc around.

Fasten off 1st Pant Leg, but do not fasten off 2nd Pant Leg.

Rnd 13 (joining): Sc around, sl st in same st as 1st sc (sl st not counted as a st), sc in middle of inner thigh of 2nd Pant Leg, sc around – 36 sc.

Rnds 14–21: Sc around.

Fasten off.

BODY

With **A**, join to center back of Pant Legs.

Rnd 1: In BLO, sc around – 36 sc.

Rnd 2: [2 sc, sc 11] x 3 – 39 sc.

Rnd 3: [Sc 6, 2 sc in next, sc 6] x 3 – 42 sc.

Rnd 4: [2 sc, sc 13] x 3 – 45 sc.

Rnd 5: [Sc 7, 2 sc in next, sc 7] x 3 – 48 sc.

Rnd 6: [2 sc, sc 15] x 3 – 51 sc.

Rnd 7: [Sc 8, 2 sc in next, sc 8] x 3 – 54 sc.

Using 2 stitch markers, mark sides of Body for Arms, ensuring there are 24 sts for front of Body and 24 sts for back of Body between markers.

Rnd 8: Sc to 1st marker, sc in marker, holding Arm join by sc 15 around Arm ensuring thumb is facing Body, sc to 2nd marked st, sc in marked st, holding 2nd Arm in line with Body and with thumb facing Body, sc 15 around Arm to join, sc in remaining sts around – 84 sc.

Rnds 9–11: Sc around.

Rnd 12: [Sc 6, invdec, sc 6] around – 78 sc.

Rnd 13: [Invdec, sc 11] around – 72 sc.

Rnd 14: [Sc 5, invdec, sc 5] around – 66 sc.

Rnd 15: [Invdec, sc 9] around – 60 sc.

Rnd 16: [Sc 4, invdec, sc 4] around – 54 sc.

Rnd 17: [Invdec, sc 7] around – 48 sc.

Rnd 18: [Sc 3, invdec, sc 3] around – 42 sc.

Rnd 19: [Invdec, sc 5] around – 36 sc.

Rnd 20: [Sc 2, invdec, sc 2] around – 30 sc.

Fasten off. Stuff Body firmly, paying attention to stuffing shoulders. Continue to Head.

HEAD

With **B**.

Rnd 1: Sc around, join – 30 sc.

Rnd 2: Ch 1 tightly, [sc 4, invdec, sc 4] around, *do not join* – 27 sc.

Rnd 3: [Invdec, sc 7] around – 24 sc.

Rnd 4: Sc around.

Rnd 5: [2 sc, sc] around – 36 sc.

Rnd 6: Fpsc around – 36 sc.

Rnds 7–19: Sc around.

Add safety eyes between Rnds 14–15 approximately 8 sts apart. Using **A**, add nose over 3 sts between Rnds 11–12. Using **D**, add eyebrows over eyes. Stuff Head and continue stuffing as work progresses.

Rnd 20: [Sc 2, invdec, sc 2] around – 30 sc.

Rnd 21: [Invdec, sc 3] around – 24 sc.

Rnd 22: [Sc, invdec, sc] around – 18 sc.

Rnd 23: [Invdec, sc] around – 12 sc.

Rnd 24: Invdec around – 6 sc.

Fasten off, leaving a long tail for sewing. Sew remaining 6 sts closed. Weave in ends.

EARS (MAKE 2)

With **A**.

Rnd 1: Ch 2, 4 sc in 2nd ch from hook.

Fasten off, leaving a long tail for sewing. Sew Ears to sides of Head in line with nose.

HAIR

With **D** and working in BLO for all rnds.

Rnd 1: Ch 2, 6 sc in 2nd ch from hook – 6 sc.

Rnd 2: 2 sc in each st around – 12 sc.

Rnd 3: [2 sc, sc in next] around – 18 sc.

Rnd 4: [Sc, 2 sc in next, sc] around – 24 sc.

Rnd 5: [2 sc, sc 3] around – 30 sc.

Rnd 6: [Sc 2, 2 sc in next, sc 2] around – 36 sc.

Rnds 7–10: Sc around.

Fasten off, leaving a long tail for sewing. Join to 1st st in FLO st left in Rnd 1.

Rnd 11 (Hair Spikes): *Ch 3, sl st in 2nd ch from hook, sc in next ch, sl st in next 4 FLO sts of Hair; rep from * around entire piece.

Sew Hair to top of Head. Weave in ends.

HEADBAND

With **B**.

Row 1: Ch 75.

Fasten off. Tie around forehead, making a knot at back of Head.

GI FRONT PANEL (MAKE 2)

With **C**.

Row 1: Ch 11, sc in 2nd ch from hook and in each across, turn – 10 sc.

Rows 2–9: Ch 1, sc across, turn.

Row 10: Ch 1, sl st 6, ch 1, sc 5, turn – 5 sc.

Rows 11–13: Ch 1, sc across, turn.

Row 14: Ch 3, sl st in 2nd ch from hook, sc in next, sc 4, turn – 5 sc.

Row 15: Ch 1, sc2tog, sc 3, turn – 4 sc.

Rows 16–17: Ch 1, sc 4, turn.

Row 18: Ch 3, sl st in 2nd ch from hook, sc in next, sc 4, turn – 5 sc.

Rows 19–20: Ch 1, sc 4 across, turn.

Row 21: Ch 1, sc2tog, sc 2, turn – 3 sc.

Row 22: Ch 3, sl st in 2nd ch from hook, sc in next, sc 3, turn – 4 sc.

Row 23: Ch 1, sc 3, turn – 3 sc.

Fasten off, leaving a long tail for sewing.

GI BACK PANEL

With **C**.

Note: The Spikes at start of rows contain a sc that is counted but not worked in proceeding rows.

Row 1: Ch 21, sc in 2nd ch from hook and in each across, turn – 20 sc.

Rows 2–9: Ch 1, sc across, turn.

Row 10: Ch 1, sl st 6, ch 1, sc 10 leaving remaining sts unworked, turn – 10 sc.

Rows 11–13: Ch 1, sc 10, turn.

Row 14: Ch 3, sl st in 2nd ch from hook, sc in next, sc 10, turn – 11 sc.

Row 15: Ch 3, sl st in 2nd ch from hook, sc in next, sc 10, turn – 11 sc.

Rows 16–17: Ch 1, sc 10, turn – 10 sc.

Rows 18–21: Rep Rows 14–17.

Rows 22–23: Rep Rows 16–17.

Fasten off, leaving a tail for sewing.

FINISHING

Seam shoulders of Gi on either side. Seam from armpit to hem on both sides. With **C**, join to inside edge of Gi and sc evenly around inside edge of Gi in row ends.

Fasten off and weave in ends. Add Gi to Body.

BELT

With **D**.

Row 1: Ch 41, sc in 2nd ch from hook, sc in each st across – 40 sc.

Fasten off, then tie around waist of Gi.

ISABELLE

SKILL LEVEL: 

Overseeing a town or island is hard work—especially when you've got no experience and just want to go catch bugs and fish! Thankfully, the hardworking Isabelle is there to offer her support in *Animal Crossing: New Leaf* and *Animal Crossing: New Horizons*, helping to take care of the day-to-day paperwork so there's more time for adventure. She's really an MVP—the most valuable pup!

FINISHED MEASUREMENTS

Height: 11 in. / 27.94 cm

Width: 6 in. / 15.24 cm

YARN

Worsted weight (#4 medium) yarn, shown in Lion Brand Yarn *Basic Stitch Anti Pilling* (100% acrylic, 185 yd. / 170 m per 3.5 oz. / 100 g skein).

Color A: #157X Lemonade, 1 skein

Color B: #126 Mahogany, 1 skein

Color D: #098C Ecru, 1 skein

Color E: #158I Mustard, 1 skein

Worsted weight (#4 medium) yarn, shown in Furls Crochet *Wander* (100% acrylic, 120 yd. / 109 m per 3.5 oz. / 100 g skein).

Color C: #0082 Sunrise, 1 skein

HOOK

US G/6 (4 mm) crochet hook

NOTIONS

Locking stitch markers

Polyester stuffing

Tapestry needle

Pair of 12 mm black safety eyes

Black embroidery thread, small amount

GAUGE

Gauge is not critical for this project. Ensure your stitches are tight so the stuffing won't show through.

SPECIAL STITCHES

Invdec (invisible single crochet decrease): Insert hook in front loop only of each of next 2 sts, yarn over and draw through both sts, yarn over and draw through 2 loops on hook – 1 st decreased.

NOTES

Work in continuous rounds unless otherwise indicated.

ARMS (MAKE 2)

With **A**.

Rnd 1: Ch 2, 6 sc in 2nd ch from hook – 6 sc.

Rnd 2: 2 sc in each st around – 12 sc.

Rnds 3–11: Sc around.

Change to **C**.

Rnd 12: Working in BLO, sc around – 12 sc.

Rnd 13: Sc around.

Fasten off. Stuff shape lightly. Set aside to join to Body.

LEGS (MAKE 2)

With **B**.

Rnd 1: Ch 2, 6 sc in 2nd ch from hook – 6 sc.

Rnd 2: 2 sc in each st around – 12 sc.

Rnd 3: Working in BLO, sc around – 12 sc.

Rnd 4: Sc around.

Change to **A**.

Rnd 5: Working in BLO, sc around – 12 sc.

Rnds 6–15: Sc around.

Stuff Leg. Fasten off 1st Leg, but do not fasten off 2nd Leg. Continue to Body.

BODY

Continuing with **A**.

Rnd 1: Ch 3, sc in 1st Leg and next 11 sts, sc 3 across underside of ch-3, sc in 12 sts of 2nd Leg – 27 sc.

Rnd 2: Sc in next 3 chs, sc around – 30 sc.

Rnd 3: [Sc 2, 2 sc in next, sc 2] around – 36 sc.

Rnds 4–9: Sc around.

Change to **C**.

Rnd 10: Working in BLO, sc around – 36 sc.

Rnds 11–15: Sc around.

Using 2 locking stitch markers, mark "armpit" st on either side of Body where Arms will be incorporated.

Rnd 16: Sc to 1st marked st, sc in marked st, sc in 12 sts of 1st Arm to incorporate, sc across to next marked st, sc in marked st, sc in 12 sts of 2nd Arm to incorporate, sc in remaining sts – 60 sc.

Rnds 17–18: Sc around.

Rnd 19: [Sc 4, invdec, sc 4] around – 54 sc.

Rnd 20: [Invdec, sc 7] around – 48 sc.

Rnd 21: [Sc 3, invdec, sc 3] around – 42 sc.

Rnd 22: [Invdec, sc 5] around – 36 sc.

Rnd 23: [Sc 2, invdec, sc 2] around – 30 sc.

Rnd 24: [Invdec, sc 3] around – 24 sc.

Fasten off **C**. Stuff Body and Arms. Continue to Head.

HEAD

With **A**, join to back of neck.

Rnd 1: Working in FLO, [2 sc, sc 3] around – 30 sc.

Rnd 2: [Sc 2, 2 sc in next, sc 2] around – 36 sc.

Rnd 3: [2 sc, sc 5] around – 42 sc.

Rnd 4: [Sc 3, 2 sc in next, sc 3] around – 48 sc.

Rnds 5–16: Sc around.

Add safety eyes between Rnds 11–12 with 5 sts between. Using black thread, embroider eyelid above eye. Using **E**, add small lines to cheeks at Rnd 8, across 3 sts on either side of face and approximately 1 st away from outer edge of eye. Stuff Head and continue stuffing as work progresses.

Rnd 17: [Sc 3, invdec, sc 3] around – 42 sc.

Rnd 18: [Invdec, sc 5] around – 36 sc.

Rnd 19: [Sc 2, invdec, sc 2] around – 30 sc.

Rnd 20: [Invdec, sc 3] around – 24 sc.

Rnd 21: [Sc, invdec, sc] around – 18 sc.

Rnd 22: [Invdec, sc] around – 12 sc.

Begin working Hairpiece.

Rnd 23: Sc around.

Rnd 24: [2sc, sc] around – 18 sc.

Rnd 25: [Sc, 2 sc in next, sc] – 24 sc.

Rnd 26: Sc around.

Rnd 27: Sc 16, leaving remaining 8 sts unworked – 16 sc.

Rnd 28: Sc around – 16 sc.

Change to **E**.

Rnd 29: Sc around – 16 sc.

Rnd 30: [Invdec, sc 2] around – 12 sc.

Rnd 31: [Invdec, sc] around – 8 sc.

Rnd 32: Invdec around – 4 sc.

Fasten off, leaving a long tail for sewing. Sew remaining 4 sts closed. Weave in ends. Stuff shape through gap made in Rnd 27.

SMALL HAIRPIECE

With **A** and leaving a long tail for sewing at start, join to any skipped st from Rnd 27 of Head.

Rnd 1: Sc around – 8 sc.

Change to **E**.

Rnd 2: Sc around.

Stuff shape.

Rnd 3: Invdec around – 4 sc.

Fasten off, leaving a long tail for sewing. Use starting tail to sew gap between Hairpiece closed. Use finishing tail to sew remaining 4 sts closed. Weave in ends.

FACE PANEL

With **D**.

Row 1: Ch 4, sc in 2nd ch from hook, sc across, turn – 3 sc.

Row 2: Ch 1, 2 sc in 1st st, sc across, 2 sc in last, turn – 5 sc.

Rows 3–4: Rep Row 2 – 9, sc at end of Row 4.

Rows 5–6: Ch 1, sc across, turn – 9 sc.

Row 7: Ch 1, sc2tog, sc across to last 2 sts, sc2tog, *do not turn* – 7 sc.

Row 8 (Edging): Rotate to sc evenly around entire piece, join.

Fasten off, leaving a long tail for sewing. Using black thread, embroider a nose at top of piece and a small mouth using photo as a guide. Sew Face Panel to Head beneath eyes and between cheek lines.

BANGS (MAKE 2)

With **A**.

Rnd 1: Ch 2, 3 sc in 2nd ch from hook – 3 sc.

Rnd 2: 2 sc in each st around – 6 sc.

Rnd 3: [2 sc, sc in next] around – 9 sc.

Rnd 4: [Sc, 2 sc in next, sc] around – 12 sc.

Rnd 5: [2 sc, sc 3] around – 15 sc.

Rnd 6: [Sc 2, 2 sc in next, sc 2] around – 18 sc.

Rnds 7–9: Sc around.

Rnd 10: [Sc, invdec] around – 12 sc.

Rnd 11: [Sc 2, invdec] around – 9 sc.

Rnd 12: [Sc, invdec] around – 6 sc.

Fasten off, leaving a long tail for sewing. Sew remaining 6 sts closed. Sew Bangs to forehead using photo as a guide.

EARS (MAKE 2)

With **E**.

Rnd 1: Ch 2, 6 sc in 2nd ch from hook – 6 sc.

Rnd 2: 2 sc in each st around – 12 sc.

Rnd 3: [2 sc, sc in next] around – 18 sc.

Rnds 4–13: Sc around.

Rnd 14: [Invdec, sc 4] around – 15 sc.

Rnd 15: [Invdec, sc 3] around – 12 sc.

Rnd 16: [Invdec, sc 2] around – 9 sc.

Rnd 17: [Invdec, sc] around – 6 sc.

Fasten off, leaving a long tail for sewing. Sew remaining 6 sts closed. Sew Ears to sides of Head, with edges overlapping the Bangs.

SKIRT

With **D**, join to back of Body in any FLO sts left from Rnd 10.

Rnds 1–8: Sc around – 36 sc.

Fasten off and weave in ends.

SHIRT HEM

With **C**.

Row 1: Ch 36.

Fasten off, leaving a long tail for sewing. Sew Hem around base of Shirt.

TAIL

With **D**.

Rnd 1: Ch 2, 3 sc in 2nd ch from hook – 3 sc.

Rnd 2: 2 sc in each st around – 6 sc.

Rnd 3: [2 sc, sc in next] around – 9 sc.

Rnd 4: [Sc, 2 sc in next, sc] around – 12 sc.

Rnd 5: Sc around.

Change to **A**.

Rnds 6–14: Sc around.

Fasten off, leaving a long tail for sewing. Stuff. Sew to back of Skirt, securing to Body.

FINISHING

Wrap a small length of **C** around base of Hairpieces. Using **D**, embroider 4 small buttons on front of Shirt. Weave in ends.

BAG OF BELLS

SKILL LEVEL: ☆

In a franchise such as *Animal Crossing*, where the entrepreneurial tanuki Tom Nook is always ready to put the player in debt, a bag of Bells is as good as gold. Serving as the currency within the franchise, Bells are typically represented by either individual coins (when in amounts less than one thousand) or bags of coins of increasing size (for large amounts). These valuable bags can be received in the mail, from villagers, or even dug up from the ground—and, under the right circumstances, planted to grow more from a tree!

FINISHED MEASUREMENTS

Height: 4.5 in. / 11.43 cm

Width: 4 in. / 10.16 cm

YARN

Worsted weight (#4 medium) yarn, shown in Lion Brand Yarn *Vanna's Choice* (100% acrylic, 170 yd. / 156 m per 3.5 oz. / 100 g skein).

Color A: #158I Mustard, 1 skein

Color B: #113 Scarlet, 1 skein

Worsted weight (#4 medium) yarn, shown in Lion Brand Yarn *Basic Stitch Anti Pilling* (100% acrylic, 185 yd. / 170 m per 3.5 oz. / 100 g skein).

Color C: #408F Russet Heather, 1 skein

HOOK

US G/6 (4 mm) crochet hook

NOTIONS

Stitch markers

Tapestry needle

Polyester stuffing

GAUGE

Gauge is not critical for this project. Ensure your stitches are tight so the stuffing won't show through.

SPECIAL STITCHES

Invdec (invisible single crochet decrease): Insert hook in front loop only of each of next 2 sts, yarn over and draw through both sts, yarn over and draw through 2 loops on hook – 1 st decreased.

NOTES

Work in continuous rounds unless otherwise indicated.

BAG

With **A**.

Rnd 1: Ch 2, 6 sc in 2nd ch from hook – 6 sc.

Rnd 2: 2 sc in each st around – 12 sc.

Rnd 3: [2 sc, sc in next] around – 18 sc.

Rnd 4: [Sc, 2 sc in next, sc] around – 24 sc.

Rnd 5: [2 sc, sc 3] around – 30 sc.

Rnd 6: [Sc 2, 2 sc in next, sc 2] around – 36 sc.

Rnd 7: [2 sc, sc 5] around – 42 sc.

Rnds 8–14: Sc around.

Rnd 15: [Invdec, sc 5] around – 36 sc.

Rnd 16: Sc around.

Rnd 17: [Sc 2, invdec, sc 2] around – 30 sc.

Rnd 18: Sc around.

Rnd 19: [Invdec, sc 3] around – 24 sc.

Rnd 20: Sc around.

Rnd 21: [Sc, invdec, sc] around – 18 sc.

Stuff firmly, and continue stuffing as work progresses.

Rnd 22: Working in BLO, sc around.

Rnd 23: [Invdec, sc] around – 12 sc.

Rnd 24: Invdec around – 6 sc.

Fasten off, leaving a long tail for sewing. Sew remaining 6 sts closed.

BAG TOP

With **A**, fasten on to any FLO st left from Rnd 22 of Bag.

Rnd 1: Ch 1, sc in each FLO around – 18 sc.

Rnd 2: [Sc, 2 sc in next, sc] around – 24 sc.

Rnd 3: Sc around.

Rnd 4: [2 sc, sc 3] around – 30 sc.

Rnd 5: Sc around.

Rnd 6: [Sc 2, 2 sc in next, sc 2] around – 36 sc.

Rnd 7: [Sc, skip next 2 sts, 5 dc in next st, skip next 2 sts] around – 30 dc, 6 sc.

Fasten off, then weave in ends.

RIBBON

With **B**.

Row 1: Leaving a long tail at start, ch 40.

Fasten off, leaving a long tail for sewing. Sew Ribbon around neck of Bag and tack down the ends of each Ribbon side.

STAR

With **C**.

Rnd 1: Ch 2, 5 sc in 2nd ch from hook, join – 5 sc.

Rnd 2: Ch 1, 2 sc in each st around, join – 10 sc.

Rnd 3: [Ch 4, sc in 2nd ch from hook, hdc in next ch, dc in last ch, skip next 2 sc on Rnd 2, sl st] around – 5 dc, 5 hdc, 5 sc.

Fasten off, leaving a long tail for sewing. Sew Star to front of Bag. Weave in ends.

KIRBY

SKILL LEVEL: 

Originally a stand-in sprite for a different character during development, Kirby has been charming everyone since the beginning—starting with when the creator of the game that would eventually become *Kirby's Dream Land* decided he was fonder of the placeholder than the intended protagonist and made Kirby the star. Since then, this pink blob's voracious appetite and versatile approach to saving the day has captured the hearts of many more, leading Kirby to star in over thirty games, with no signs of stopping.

FINISHED MEASUREMENTS

Height: 4 in. / 10.16 cm

Width: 5 in. / 12.7 cm

YARN

Worsted weight (#4 medium) yarn, shown in WeCrochet *Brava Worsted* (100% acrylic, 218 yd. / 199 m per 3.5 oz. / 100 g skein).

Color A: Cotton Candy, 1 skein

Color B: Red, 1 skein

DK weight (#3 light) yarn, shown in WeCrochet *Palette* (100% wool, 231 yd. / 211 m per 1.75 oz. / 50 g skein).

Color C: Black, small amount

Color D: Whirlpool, small amount

Color E: Rose Hip, small amount

Color F: Tea Rose, small amount

HOOKS

US G/6 (4 mm) crochet hook

US 1.5 mm steel crochet hook

NOTIONS

Stitch markers

Polyester stuffing

Tapestry needle

Black and white felt, small amounts

Fabric glue

GAUGE

Gauge is not critical for this project. Ensure your stitches are tight so the stuffing won't show through.

SPECIAL STITCHES

Invdec (invisible single crochet decrease): Insert hook in front loop only of each of next 2 sts, yarn over and draw through both sts, yarn over and draw through 2 loops on hook – 1 st decreased.

NOTES

Work in continuous rounds unless otherwise indicated.

BODY

With **A** and larger hook.

Rnd 1: Ch 2, 6 sc in 2nd ch from hook – 6 sc.

Rnd 2: 2 sc in each st around – 12 sc.

Rnd 3: [Sc, 2 sc in next, sc] around – 18 sc.

Rnd 4: [2 sc, sc 3] around – 30 sc.

Rnd 5: [Sc 2, 2 sc in next, sc 2] around – 36 sc.

Rnd 6: [2 sc, sc 5] around – 42 sc.

Rnd 7: [Sc 3, 2 sc in next, sc 3] around – 48 sc.

Rnd 8: [2 sc, sc 7] around – 54 sc.

Rnds 9–17: Sc around.

Rnd 18: [Invdec, sc 7] around – 48 sc.

Rnd 19: [Sc 3, invdec, sc 3] around – 42 sc.

Rnd 20: [Invdec, sc 5] around – 36 sc.

Rnd 21: [Sc 2, invdec, sc 2] around – 30 sc.

Rnd 22: [Invdec, sc 3] around – 24 sc.

Stuff Body. Continue stuffing as work progresses.

Rnd 23: [Sc, invdec, sc] around – 18 sc.

Rnd 24: [Invdec, sc] around – 12 sc.

Rnd 25: Invdec around – 6 sc.

Fasten off, leaving a long tail for sewing. Sew remaining 6 sts closed. Weave in ends.

ARMS (MAKE 2)

With **A** and larger hook.

Rnd 1: Ch 2, 6 sc in 2nd ch from hook – 6 sc.

Rnd 2: 2 sc in each st around – 12 sc.

Rnd 3: [2 sc, sc 3] around – 15 sc.

Rnds 4–5: Sc around.

Fasten off, leaving a long tail for sewing. Stuff Arms. Sew left Arm between Rnds 11–16 of Body. Sew right Arm between Rnds 8–14 of Body.

SHOES (MAKE 2)

With **B** and larger hook.

Rnd 1: Ch 9, sc 7, 3 sc in last ch, rotate to work on underside of ch, sc 7, 3 sc in last – 20 sc.

Rnd 2: [Sc 7, 2 sc in next 3 sts] x 2 – 26 sc.

Rnd 3: Working in BLO, sc around.

Rnd 4: Sc 7, [hdc2tog] x 3, sc 13 – 23 sts.

Rnd 5: Sc 4, [hdc3tog] x 3, sc 10 – 17 sts.

Fasten off, leaving a long tail for sewing. Stuff Shoes lightly, ensuring not to stretch out the stitches. Sew Shoes to bottom of Body using photo as a guide.

EYES (MAKE 2)

With **C** and smaller hook.

Rnd 1: Ch 6, sc 4, change to **D**, 3 sc with **D** in last ch, change to **C**, rotate to work on underside of ch, sc 4, 3 sc in last ch, join – 14 sc.

Fasten off, leaving a long tail for sewing. Sew Eye with blue portion facing down between Rnds 5–10 of Body, with 3 sc between inside edges of Eyes. Add a small circle of white felt to top of Eye.

CHEEKS (MAKE 2)

With **E** and smaller hook.

Rnd 1: Rep Rnd 1 of Eye, omitting any color changes.

Fasten off, leaving a long tail for sewing. Sew Cheeks 1 rnd below Eyes and off to each side, using photo as a guide.

MOUTH

With **E** and smaller hook.

Row 1: Ch 2, 3 sc in 2nd ch from hook, turn – 3 sc.

Row 2: Ch 1, sc, 2 sc in next, sc in last, turn – 4 sc.

Change to **F**.

Row 3: Ch 1, hdc, 2 hdc in next 2 sts, hdc in last – 6 hdc.

Fasten off and weave in ends. Glue Mouth to a piece of black felt and trim edges. Glue Mouth to Body between Eyes and 1 rnd below.

FREDDY

SKILL LEVEL: ★ ★ ★

Once the face and star attraction of the Freddy Fazbear's Pizza Place, the now-terrifying animatronic bear Freddy has fallen into disrepair after the pizzeria was abandoned following some . . . concerning events. This titular character of the *Five Nights at Freddy's* franchise wanders the restaurant at night, taking advantage of the shadows as he stalks the nighttime security guard alongside the rest of his haunted band.

FINISHED MEASUREMENTS

Height: 13 in. / 33.02 cm

Width: 9 in. / 22.86 cm

YARN

Worsted weight (#4 medium) yarn, shown in Lion Brand Yarn *Basic Stitch Anti Pilling* (100% acrylic, 185 yd. / 170 m per 3.5 oz. / 100 g skein).

Color A: #126AL Mahogany, 1 skein

Color B: #404J Silver Heather, 1 skein

Color C: #125AA Truffle, 1 skein

Color D: #153 Black, 1 skein

Color E: #100, White, 1 skein

HOOK

US G/6 (4 mm) crochet hook

NOTIONS

Stitch markers

Tapestry needle

Polyester stuffing

Two bamboo rods

Black, white, and blue felt, small amounts

Pair of 6 mm black safety eyes

Black embroidery thread, small amount

GAUGE

Gauge is not critical for this project. Ensure your stitches are tight so the stuffing won't show through.

SPECIAL STITCHES

Invdec (invisible single crochet decrease): Insert hook in front loop only of each of next 2 sts, yarn over and draw through both sts, yarn over and draw through 2 loops on hook – 1 st decreased.

NOTES

Work in continuous rounds unless otherwise indicated.

TOES (MAKE 6)

With **A**, make a magic ring.

Rnd 1: Sc 3 in ring – 3 sc.

Rnd 2: 2 sc in each st around – 6 sc.

Rnd 3: Sc around – 6 sc.

Fasten off. Continue to Foot.

FEET (MAKE 2)

With **A** and joining 3 Toes per Foot.

Rnd 1: Join to 1st Toe, sc 3, sc 3 on 2nd Toe, sc 6 around 3rd Toe, rotate to sc 3 on 2nd Toe, sc 3 on 1st Toe – 18 sc.

Rnd 2: Sc around.

Rnd 3: [Sc 2, invdec, sc 2] around – 15 sc.

Rnd 4: [Invdec, sc 3] around – 12 sc.

Rnd 5: Ch 6, skip 6 sts (*ankle opening made*), sc 6 – 6 sc.

Rnd 6: Sc in next 6 chs, sc 6 – 12 sc.

Rnd 7: Invdec around – 6 sc.

Fasten off, leaving a long tail for sewing. Sew remaining 6 sts closed. Weave in end. Continue to Legs.

LEGS (MAKE 2)

With **A**, join to 1st skipped sc of Rnd 5 of Foot.

Rnd 1: Sc 6, sc in gap before underside of next ch, sc 6 across underside of ch-6, sc in gap before 1st sc made – 14 sc.

Rnd 2: [Sc 5, invdec] around – 12 sc.

Rnd 3: Invdec around – 6 sc.

Stuff back of Foot, but do not stuff Toe area.

Rnd 4: Sc around.

Rnd 5: 3 sc in each st around – 18 sc.

Rnds 6–13: Sc around.

Stuff Leg, but do not overstuff. Piece should squish into a squat cylinder.

Rnd 14: Invdec around – 9 sc.

Rnd 15: [Sc, invdec] around – 6 sc.

Rnds 16–27: Rep Rnds 4–15.

Rnd 28: Sc around – 6 sc.

Fasten off.

KNEE JOINTS (MAKE 2)

With **A**.

Rnd 1: Ch 4, sl st to form a ring, ch 1, sc 4 – 4 sc.

Rnds 2–7: Sc around.

Fasten off, leaving a long tail for sewing. Sew Knee Joints around gap for each knee. Weave in ends.

LEG JOINTS (MAKE 4)

With **B**.

Row 1: Ch 7, sc in 2nd ch from hook and in each across – 6 sc.

Fasten off, leaving a long tail for sewing. Sew a Joint to each ankle, and Joints to h p in the decrease. Weave in ends.

BODY

With **A**, make a magic ring.

Rnd 1: Sc 6 in ring – 6 sc.

Rnd 2: 2 sc in each st around – 12 sc.

Rnd 3: [2 sc, sc 3] around – 15 sc.

Rnd 4: [Sc 2, 2 sc, sc 2] around – 18 sc.

Rnd 5: [2 sc, sc 2] around – 24 sc.

Rnd 6: [2 sc, sc 3] around – 30 sc.

Rnd 7: [Sc 2, 2 sc, sc 2] around – 36 sc.

Rnd 8: *Sc 18, holding Leg in line with Body sc 6 on Leg; rep from * around – 48 sc.

Rnds 9–11: Sc around.

Rnd 12: In BLO, sc around.

Insert a bamboo rod into each Leg for support.

Rnds 13–15: Sc around – 48 sc.

Rnd 16: [Invdec, sc 14] around – 45 sc.

Rnds 17–19: Sc around.

Rnd 20: [Invdec, sc 13] around – 42 sc.

Rnds 21–23: Sc around.

Rnd 24: [Invdec, sc 12] around – 39 sc.

Rnds 25–27: Sc around.

Rnd 28: [Sc, invdec] around – 26 sc.

Rnd 29: *Sc, [invdec] x 6; rep from * around – 14 sc.

Rnd 30: [Invdec, sc 5] x 2 – 12 sc.

Rnd 31: 3 sc in each st around – 36 sc.

Rnds 32–36: Sc around.

Rnd 37: 2 sc in next 24 sts, sc 12 – 60 sc.

Rnds 38–40: Sc around.

Rnd 41: [Sc 4, invdec, sc 4] around – 54 sc.

Rnd 42: [Invdec, sc 7] around – 48 sc.

Rnd 43: [Sc 3, invdec, sc 3] around – 42 sc.

Rnds 44–49: Sc around.

Rnd 50: [Invdec, sc 5] around – 36 sc.

Rnd 51: [Sc 2, invdec, sc 2] around – 30 sc.

Rnd 52: [Invdec, sc 3] around – 24 sc.

Using black, white, and blue felt, and with photos as a guide, add felt layers to back of safety eyes. Add eyes between Rnds 45–46. Stuff. Continue to Hat.

HAT

With **D**, join to back of Head in Rnd 52.

Rnd 1: Ch 1, sc around, join – 24 sc.

Rnd 2: Ch 1, working in BLO, sc around.

Rnds 3–6: Ch 1, sc around, join.

Fasten off and stuff Hat. Continue to Hat Top.

HAT TOP

With **D**, make a magic ring.

Rnd 1: 6 sc in ring – 6 sc.

Rnd 2: 2 sc in each st around – 12 sc.

Rnd 3: [2 sc, sc] around – 18 sc.

Rnd 4: [Sc, 2 sc, sc] around – 24 sc.

Fasten off, leaving a long tail for sewing. Sew Hat Top to opening at top of Hat. Weave in ends.

HAT BRIM

With **D**, join to back of Hat in FLO sts of Rnd 2 of Hat.

Rnd 1: Ch 1, [2 sc, sc 3] around, join – 30 sc.

Fasten off and weave in ends.

JAW

With **A**.

Rnd 1: Ch 9, sc in 2nd ch from hook, sc 6, 3 sc in last, rotate to work in underside of ch, sc 7, 3 sc in last – 20 sc.

Rnd 2: *Sc 7, 2 sc in next 3 sc; rep from * around – 26 sc.

Rnds 3–5: Sc around.

Fasten off, leaving a long tail for sewing. Stuff piece lightly. Sew piece shut lengthwise, joining each side of Rnd 5. Sew Jaw to bottom of Head. Weave in ends.

FACE PAD (MAKE 2)

With **C**.

Row 1: Ch 2, 3 sc in 2nd ch from hook, turn – 3 sc.

Row 2: Ch 1, 2 sc in each st, turn – 6 sc.

Row 3: Ch 1, [2 sc, sc] across, *do not turn* – 9 sc.

Row 4: Ch 1, rotate to work across row ends, sc 7 evenly across row ends, turn – 7 sc.

Rows 5–7: Ch 1, sc across, turn.

Fasten off, leaving a long tail for sewing. Sew Row 7 of each piece together in BLO. Sew piece to face above Jaw. Weave in ends. Using **D**, add 3 freckles to each side of Face Pad.

NOSE

With **D**, make a magic ring.

Rnd 1: 6 sc in ring – 6 sc.

Rnd 2: [2 sc, sc 2] around – 8 sc.

Fasten off, leaving a long tail for sewing. Sew Nose to top of Face Pad.

EYEBROWS (MAKE 2)

With **D**.

Row 1: Ch 5, sl st in 2nd ch from hook, sc 2, hdc in last – 4 sts.

Fasten off, leaving a long tail for sewing. Using photos as a guide, sew Eyebrows above eyes. Weave in ends.

EARS (MAKE 2)

With **A**, make a magic ring.

Rnd 1: 6 sc in ring – 6 sc.

Rnd 2: 2 sc in each st around – 12 sc.

Rnds 3–6: Sc around.

Rnd 7: Invdec around – 6 sc.

Rnd 8: Sc around.

Fasten off, leaving a long tail for sewing. Flatten shape. Sew each Ear to sides of Head, 2 rnds below edge of Hat. Weave in ends.

EAR JOINTS (MAKE 2)

Rep as per Leg Joints.

Fasten off, leaving a long tail for sewing. Sew to base of Ears.

TEETH

With **E**.

Row 1: Ch 11, sc in 2nd ch from hook and in each across, turn – 10 sc.

Fasten off, leaving a long tail for sewing. Using black thread, embroider Teeth gaps using photos as a guide. Sew to inside of mouth between Jaw and Face Pad. Weave in ends.

BELLY PATCH

With **C**.

Row 1: Ch 13, sc in 2nd ch from hook and in each across, turn – 12 sc.

Rows 2–10: Ch 1, sc across, turn.

Row 11: Ch 1, sc, sc2tog, sc 6, sc2tog, sc in last, turn – 10 sc.

Row 12: Ch 1, sc, sc2tog, sc 4, sc2tog, sc in last, turn – 8 sc.

Row 13: Ch 1, sc, sc2tog, sc 2, sc2tog, sc in last, *do not turn*, ch 1, rotate to work in row ends, sc 12 across row ends, ch 1, sc 12 across bottom, ch 1, sc 12 across opposite edge row ends, join – 42 sc.

Fasten off, leaving a long tail for sewing. Sew Belly Patch to front of Body, with bottom of Patch meeting Rnd 12 FLO sts.

BOW TIE (MAKE 2)

With **D**, leave a long tail at start for sewing.

Row 1: Ch 2, 2 sc in 2nd ch from hook, turn – 2 sc.

Row 2: Ch 1, 2 sc in each across, turn – 4 sc.

Row 3: Ch 1, (sc, dc) in 1st st, (dc, sl st) in next st, (sl st, dc) in next st, (dc, sc) in last st – 8 sts.

Fasten off, then sew in end. Using starting tail, sew 2 pieces together at Row 1. Using starting tail, wrap center of Bow Tie 3 times and secure with a knot. Sew Bow Tie to top of Body at neck. Weave in ends.

THUMBS (MAKE 2)

With **A**, make a magic ring.

Rnd 1: 4 sc in ring – 4 sc.

Rnds 2–3: Sc around.

Fasten off and continue to Hands.

HANDS (MAKE 2)

With **A**, make a magic ring.

Rnd 1: 6 sc in ring – 6 sc.

Rnd 2: 2 sc in each around – 12 sc.

Rnds 3–4: Sc around.

Rnd 5: Holding Thumb in line with sts, sc 4 around Thumb, sc 12 around Hand – 16 sc.

Rnds 6–8: Sc around.

Rnd 9: [Invdec, sc 2] around – 12 sc.

Rnd 10: Invdec around – 6 sc.

Rnd 11: Sc around.

Rnd 12: 3 sc in each st around – 18 sc.

Rnds 13–18: Sc around.

Rnd 19: Invdec around – 9 sc.

Stuff shape lightly.

Rnd 20: [Sc, invdec] around – 6 sc.

Rnd 21: Sc around

Rnd 22: 3 sc in each st around – 18 sc.

Rnds 23–30: Sc around.

Rnd 31: Invdec around – 9 sc.

Fasten off. Stuff lightly. Continue to Shoulder Tops.

SHOULDER TOPS (MAKE 2)

With **A**, make a magic ring.

Rnd 1: 6 sc in ring – 6 sc.

Rnd 2: 2 sc in each st around – 12 sc.

Fasten off, leaving a long tail for sewing. Using 2 stitch markers, mark 3 sts on inside edge of Arm (armpit) where Arm will meet Body, ensuring the Thumb is facing the Body for left and right Arm. Sew Shoulder Top to top of each Arm, facing in the correct direction on either side of marked sts, leaving 6 sts on Shoulder Top unsewn. This leaves 3 sc on Arm in armpit and 6 sc left on Shoulder Top. Join with **A** in 1st of 3 sc on Arm.

Rnd 3: Ch 1, sc 3 in 3 sts of Arm, 2 sc in gap before 6 Shoulder sts, sc 6 on Shoulder, 2 sc in gap before 1st sc made, join – 13 sc.

Fasten off, leaving a long tail for sewing. Stuff Shoulder Top lightly. Sew Arm to top of Body. Weave in ends.

MICROPHONE

With **B**, make a magic ring.

Rnd 1: 6 sc in ring, join – 6 sc.

Rnd 2: Ch 1, 2 sc in each st around, join – 12 sc.

Rnd 3: Ch 1, sc around, join.

Rnd 4: Ch 1, working in BLO sc around, join – 12 sc.

Rnd 5: Ch 1, invdec around, join – 6 sc.

Change to **D**.

Rnds 6–11: Ch 1, sc around, join – 6 sc.

Fasten off and stuff. Weave in ends.

MICROPHONE TIP

With **D**, make a magic ring.

Rnd 1: 6 sc in ring, join – 6 sc.

Fasten off, leaving a long tail for sewing. Sew Microphone Tip to bottom of Microphone. Weave in ends. Sew Microphone to right Hand.

PIKMIN

SKILL LEVEL: ☆

Delightful little plantlike creatures that call the planet PNF-404 home, Pikmin come in many colors, with each variety having its own unique skill set. While they may be small and fairly weak on their own, in large numbers they can accomplish great tasks. With their help, Captain Olimar has been able to survive several journeys (both intentional and not) to PNF-404, befriending the Pikmin he meets throughout each *Pikmin* game.

FINISHED MEASUREMENTS

Height: 11 in. / 27.94 cm

Width: 6.5 in. / 16.51 cm

YARN

Worsted weight (#4 medium) yarn, shown in Lion Brand Yarn *Basic Stitch Anti Pilling* (100% acrylic, 185 yd. / 170 m per 3.5 oz. / 100 g skein).

Color A: #157X Lemonade, 1 skein

Color B: #100 White, 1 skein

HOOK

US G/6 (4 mm) crochet hook

NOTIONS

Stitch markers

Tapestry needle

Polyester stuffing

Pair of 6 mm black safety eyes

White felt, small amount

SPECIAL STITCHES

Invdec (invisible single crochet decrease): Insert hook in front loop only of each of next 2 sts, yarn over and draw through both sts, yarn over and draw through 2 loops on hook – 1 st decreased.

NOTES

Work in continuous rounds unless otherwise indicated.

ARMS (MAKE 2)

With **A**.

Rnd 1: Ch 2, 6 sc in 2nd ch from hook – 6 sc.

Rnd 2: Working in BLO, sc around – 6 sc.

Rnd 3: [2 sc, sc in next] around – 9 sc.

Rnds 4–8: Sc around.

Fasten off and weave in ends. Stuff. Set aside to join to Body.

FEET (MAKE 2)

With **A**.

Rnd 1: Ch 2, 6 sc in 2nd ch from hook – 6 sc.

Rnd 2: Working in BLO, sc around – 6 sc.

Rnd 3: 2 sc in each st around – 12 sc.

Fasten off 1st Foot, but do not fasten off 2nd Foot. Continue to Body.

BODY

With **A**.

Rnd 1: Ch 3, sc 12 around 1st Foot, sc across underside of ch-3, sc 12 around 2nd Foot, sc across opposite side of ch-3 – 30 sc.

Rnd 2: [Sc 2, 2 sc in next, sc 2] around – 36 sc.

Rnd 3: [2 sc, sc 5] around – 42 sc.

Rnds 4–8: Sc around.

Using 2 stitch markers, mark armpit at each side of Body, leaving 20 sts for front of Body and 20 sts for back of Body between stitch markers.

Rnd 9: Sc to 1st marked st, sc in marked st, incorporate 1st Arm by sc 9 around Arm, continue working on Body by sc in sts until next marked st, sc in marked st, incorporate 2nd Arm by sc 9 around Arm, sc in remaining sts – 60 sc.

Rnd 10: [Sc 4, invdec, sc 4] around – 54 sc.

Rnd 11: [Invdec, sc 7] around – 48 sc.

Rnd 12: [Sc 3, invdec, sc 3] around – 42 sc.

Stuff Body. Continue stuffing as work progresses.

Rnd 13: [Sc 6, invdec, sc 6] around – 39 sc.

Rnd 14: [Invdec, sc 11] around – 36 sc.

Rnd 15: [Sc 5, invdec, sc 5] around – 33 sc.

Rnd 16: [Invdec, sc 9] around – 30 sc.

Rnd 17: [Sc 4, invdec, sc 4] around – 27 sc.

Rnd 18: [Invdec, sc 7] around – 24 sc.

Continue to Head.

HEAD

Continuing with **A**.

Rnd 1: Working in BLO, [2 sc, sc 3] around – 30 sc.

Rnd 2: [Sc 2, 2 sc, sc 2] around – 36 sc.

Rnd 3: [2 sc, sc 5] around – 42 sc.

Rnds 4–10: Sc around.

Rnd 11: [Invdec, sc 5] around – 36 sc.

Rnd 12: [Sc 2, invdec, sc 2] around – 30 sc.

Add a small oval of white felt to the back of each safety eye. Add safety eyes between Rnds 8–11 using photo as a guide.

Stuff Body and Head. Continue stuffing as work progresses.

Rnd 13: [Invdec, sc 3] around – 24 sc.

Rnd 14: [Sc, invdec, sc] around – 18 sc.

Rnd 15: [Invdec, sc] around – 12 sc.

Rnds 16–26: Sc around.

Rnd 27: [Invdec, sc 2] around – 9 sc.

Rnds 28–37: Sc around.

Rnd 38: Working in BLO, sc around.

Rnd 39: [2 sc, sc 3] around – 12 sc.

Rnd 40: [2 sc, sc] around – 18 sc.

Rnds 41–42: Sc around.

Stuff.

Rnd 43: [Invdec, sc] around – 12 sc.

Rnd 44: Invdec around – 6 sc.

Fasten off, leaving a long tail for sewing. Sew remaining 6 sts closed. Weave in ends.

EARS (MAKE 2)

With **A**.

Rnd 1: Ch 2, 4 sc in 2nd ch from hook – 4 sc.

Rnd 2: [2 sc, sc in next] around – 6 sc.

Rnd 3: [2 sc, sc 2] around – 8 sc.

Rnd 4: [2 sc, sc 3] around – 10 sc.

Rnd 5: [2 sc, sc 4] around – 12 sc.

Rnd 6: [2 sc, sc 5] around – 14 sc.

Rnds 7–12: Sc around.

Fasten off, leaving a long tail for sewing. Sew Ears to sides of Head using photo as a guide.

FLOWER PETALS (MAKE 5)

With **B**.

Rnd 1: Ch 2, 6 sc in 2nd ch from hook – 6 sc.

Rnd 2: 2 sc in each st around – 12 sc.

Rnds 3–4: Sc around.

Rnd 5: [Invdec, sc 4] around – 10 sc.

Rnd 6: [Invdec, sc 3] around – 8 sc.

Rnd 7: [Invdec, sc 2] around – 6 sc.

Rnd 8: [Invdec, sc] around – 3 sc.

Fasten off, leaving a long tail for sewing. Sew Flower Petals to FLO sts left over from Rnd 38 of Head. Weave in ends.

MURLOC

SKILL LEVEL: ★★★

Recently appearing on the shorelines of Azeroth and even venturing inland to freshwater areas, Murlocs have become a common sight on all continents. In fact, you can hardly go anywhere in *World of Warcraft* without seeing these little guys running around excitedly, fishing, or talking with their fellows. Hardy and adaptable, this amphibious race has remained unknown for a long time. While they are intelligent and capable of speaking a common language with other races, they tend to keep to themselves, shunning other races and sticking with their distinctive language. *Mglrmglmglmgl!*

FINISHED MEASUREMENTS

Height: 6.5 in. / 16.51 cm

Width: 9 in. / 22.86 cm

YARN

Worsted weight (#4 medium) yarn, shown in Lion Brand Yarn *Vanna's Choice* (100% acrylic, 170 yd. / 156 m per 3.5 oz. / 100 g skein).

Color A: #113 Scarlet, 1 skein

Worsted weight (#4 medium) yarn, shown in Lion Brand Yarn *Basic Stitch Anti Pilling* (100% acrylic, 185 yd. / 170 m per 3.5 oz. / 100 g skein).

Color B: #130B Grass, 1 skein

Color C: #153 Black, 1 skein

Color D: #100 White, 1 skein

HOOK

US G/6 (4 mm) crochet hook

NOTIONS

Tapestry needle

Polyester stuffing

Stitch markers

Red felt, small amount

Pair of 15 mm black safety eyes

GAUGE

Gauge is not critical for this project. Ensure your stitches are tight so the stuffing won't show through.

SPECIAL STITCHES

Invdec (invisible single crochet decrease): Insert hook in front loop only of each of next 2 sts, yarn over and draw through both sts, yarn over and draw through 2 loops on hook – 1 st decreased.

NOTES

Work in continuous rounds unless otherwise indicated.

THUMBS (MAKE 2)

With **A**, make a magic ring.

Rnd 1: 5 sc in ring – 5 sc.

Rnds 2–4: Sc around.

Fasten off and set aside for Hands.

FINGERS / TOES (MAKE 10)

With **A**, make a magic ring.

Rnds 1–4: Rep as per Thumbs.

Rnd 5: Sc around.

Fasten off and set 4 aside for Hands. Set 6 aside for Feet.

HANDS (MAKE 2)

With **A**, stitch around 2 Fingers to join them together.

Rnd 1: Sc 3 on 1st Finger, sc 5 around 2nd Finger, rotate to sc 2 on 1st Finger – 10 sc.

Rnds 2–3: Sc around – 10 sc.

Rnd 4 (incorporate Thumb): Sc 5 around Thumb, sc 10 – 15 sc.

Rnd 5: Sc around.

Rnd 6: [Invdec, sc 3] around – 12 sc.

Fasten off and continue to Arms.

ARMS (MAKE 2)

With **B**, join to any st of Hand in BLO.

Rnd 1: Working in BLO, sc around – 12 sc.

Rnd 2: Ch 1 tightly, sc around, *do not join* – 12 sc.

Rnds 3–10: Sc around.

Rnd 11: [2 sc, sc 3] around – 15 sc.

Rnds 12–13: Sc around.

Rnd 14: [2 sc, sc 4] around – 18 sc.

Rnds 15–18: Sc around.

Fasten off and weave in ends. Stuff Arms. Set aside to join to Body.

FEET (MAKE 2)

With **A**, stitch around 3 Toes to join them together.

Rnd 1: Sc 3 on 1st Toe, sc 2 on 2nd Toe, sc 5 around 3rd Toe, rotate to sc 3 on 2nd Toe, sc 2 on 1st Toe – 15 sc.

Rnds 2–3: Sc around.

Rnd 4: Sc, ch 6, skip next 6 sts (*leg hole made*), sc 8 – 9 sc.

Rnd 5: Sc in each sc and ch around – 15 sc.

Rnd 6: [Invdec, sc 3] around – 12 sc.

Rnd 7: Invdec around – 6 sc.

Fasten off, leaving a tail for sewing. Sew 6 remaining sts closed. Weave in ends.

With **A**, join to 1st skipped st of Rnd 4.

Rnd 8 (Ankle): Sc 6 in skipped sts, sc in gap between last sc made and underside of ch-6, sc in underside of next 6 chs, sc in gap before 1st sc of rnd, join – 14 sc.

Fasten off. Stuff Foot lightly. Continue to Legs.

LEGS (MAKE 2)

With **B**, join to back of heel.

Note: This section alternates between short rows and rounds.

Rnd 1: Working in BLO, sc around – 12 sc.

Rnds 2–9: Sc around.

Adjust start of rnd by placing a marker in inner thigh at side of Leg. Marker is new beginning of rnd. Sc to marker.

Row 10: Sc 6, turn – 6 sc.

Row 11: Ch 1 tightly, sc 6, turn – 6 sc.

Rnd 12: Ch 1 tightly, sc 6, sc in skipped 6 sts from 3 rows below – 12 sc.

Rnd 13: Sc around – 12 sc.

Rnd 14: [2 sc, sc 3] around – 15 sc.

Row 15: Sc 8, turn – 8 sc.

Row 16: Ch 1 tightly, sc 8, turn – 8 sc.

Rnd 17: Ch 1 tightly, sc 8, sc in skipped 7 sts from 3 rows below – 15 sc.

Rnd 18: Sc around – 15 sc.

Rnd 19: [Sc 2, 2 sc, sc 2] around – 18 sc.

Rnds 20–22: Sc around.

Fasten off, leaving a long tail for sewing. Stuff Leg.

BODY

With **B**.

Note: This section alternates between short rows and rounds.

Rnd 1: Ch 36, sl st to form a ring, sc in each ch around – 36 sc.

Row 2: Sc 18, turn – 18 sc.

Row 3: Ch 1 tightly, sc 18, turn – 18 sc.

Rnd 4: Ch 1 tightly, sc 18, sc 18 in skipped sts from 3 rows below – 36 sc.

Rnd 5: Sc around.

Rows/Rnds 6–17: Rep Rows/Rnds 2–5.

Rnd 18 (incorporate Arms): Sc 18, sc 18 around 1st Arm ensuring Thumb faces Body, sc 18 on Body, sc 18 on 2nd Arm ensuring Thumb faces Body – 72 sc.

Stuff tops of Arms as work progresses.

Rnd 19: *Sc 18, [invdec, sc] x 6; rep from * around – 60 sc.

Rnd 20: *Sc 18, [invdec] x 6; rep from * around – 48 sc.

Rnd 21: Sc around – 48 sc.

Row 22: Sc 18, turn – 18 sc.

Row 23: Ch 1 tightly, sc 18, turn – 18 sc.

Rnd 24: Ch 1 tightly, sc 18, sc 30 in skipped sts from 3 rows below – 48 sc.

Rnd 25: Sc around.

Rows/Rnds 26–29: Rep Rows/Rnds 22–25.

Row 30: Sc 20, turn – 20 sc.

Row 31: Ch 1 tightly, sc 20, turn – 20 sc.

Rnd 32: Ch 1 tightly, sc 20, sc 28 in skipped sts from 3 rows below – 48 sc.

Rnd 33: Sc around.

Rows/Rnds 34–37: Rep Rows/Rnds 29–33.

Rnd 38: [Sc 3, invdec, sc 3] around – 42 sc.

Rnd 39: [Invdec, 5] around – 36 sc.

Rnd 40: [Sc 2, invdec, sc 2] around – 30 sc.

Rnd 41: [Invdec, sc 3] around – 24 sc.

Rnd 42: [Sc, invdec, sc] around – 18 sc.

Rnd 43: [Invdec, sc] around – 12 sc.

Rnd 44: Invdec around – 6 sc.

Fasten off, leaving a long tail for sewing. Sew remaining 6 sts closed. Weave in ends. Stuff Body. Add Legs to back of Body. Add red felt to back of eyes. Add eyes between Rows 5–6, approximately 3 sts apart. Add nostrils between eyes with **C**. Using photo as a guide and with **D**, embroider shapes across spine, changing to **A**.

Rnd 45: With **B**, join to underside of starting ch, ch 1 tightly, sc in each ch around, join – 36 sc.

Fasten off, leaving a long tail for sewing.

BELLY PATCH (MAKE 2)

With **D**.

Row 1: Ch 2, 3 sc in 2nd ch from hook, turn – 3 sc.

Row 2: Ch 1, 2 sc in each st across, turn – 6 sc.

Row 3: Ch 1, [2 sc, sc in next] across, turn – 9 sc.

Row 4: Ch 1, [2 sc, sc 2] across, turn – 12 sc.

Row 5: Ch 1, [2 sc, sc 3] across, turn – 15 sc.

Row 6: Ch 1, [2 sc, sc 4] across, *do not turn* – 18 sc.

Row 7: Ch 1, rotate to work across row ends, sc 18 evenly across row ends, turn – 18 sc.

Rows 8–11: Ch 1, sc across, turn.

Fasten off, leaving a long tail for sewing. Join 2 pieces by sewing both edges of Row 11 together. Sew Belly Patch to bottom of Body. Weave in ends.

SPIKES (MAKE 8)

With **A**.

Row 1: Ch 11, sc in 2nd ch from hook and in each ch across – 10 sc.

Fasten off, leaving a long tail for sewing. Sew Spikes down back of Body, with 4 Spikes on either side of spine. Weave in ends.

MOUTH

With **C**.

Rnd 1: Ch 2, 6 sc in 2nd ch from hook – 6 sc.

Rnd 2: 2 sc in each st around – 12 sc.

Rnd 3: [2 sc, sc in next] around – 18 sc.

Rnd 4: [Sc, 2 sc in next, sc] around – 24 sc.

Rnd 5: [2 sc, sc 3] around – 30 sc.

Rnd 6: [Sc 2, 2 sc in next, sc 2] around – 36 sc.

TEETH

With **D**.

Working in FLO of Rnd 6 of Mouth, join to any st around.

Rnd 1: *Ch 3, sl st in 3rd ch from hook, sc in next ch, skip next st on Rnd 6 of Mouth, sl st in next 2 sts; rep from * around, join – 12 Teeth.

Fasten off and weave in ends.

FINISHING

Sew Mouth to opening of Body using tail from Body.

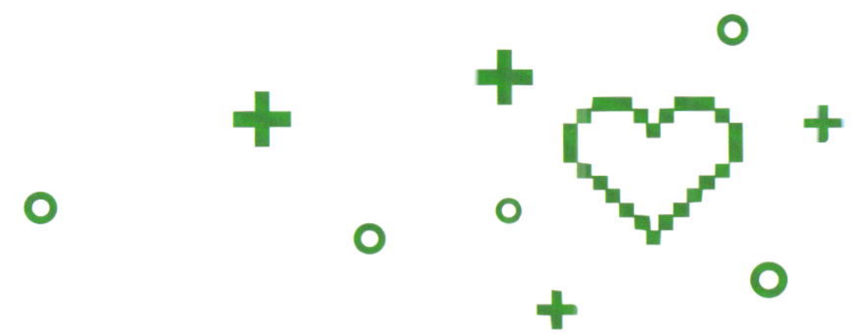

BLUE CHICKEN

SKILL LEVEL: ⭐

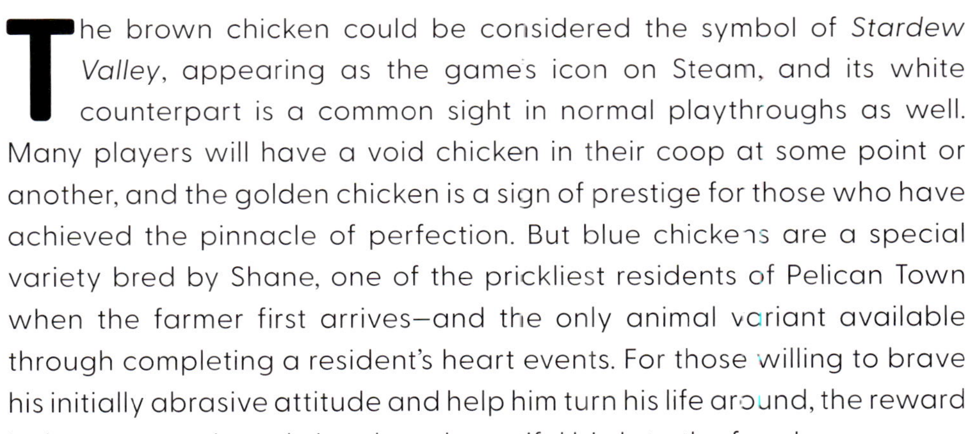

The brown chicken could be considered the symbol of *Stardew Valley*, appearing as the game's icon on Steam, and its white counterpart is a common sight in normal playthroughs as well. Many players will have a void chicken in their coop at some point or another, and the golden chicken is a sign of prestige for those who have achieved the pinnacle of perfection. But blue chickens are a special variety bred by Shane, one of the prickliest residents of Pelican Town when the farmer first arrives—and the only animal variant available through completing a resident's heart events. For those willing to brave his initially abrasive attitude and help him turn his life around, the reward is the opportunity to bring these beautiful birds to the farm!

FINISHED MEASUREMENTS

Height: 4 in. / 10.16 cm

Width: 4 in. / 10.16 cm

YARN

Worsted weight (#4 medium) yarn, shown in Furls Crochet *Wander* (100% acrylic, 120 yd. / 109 m per 3.5 oz. / 100 g skein).

Color A: Caspian, 1 skein

Color B: Orchid, 1 skein

Color C: Ambrosia, 1 skein

HOOK

US G/6 (4 mm) crochet hook

NOTIONS

Stitch markers

Tapestry needle

Polyester stuffing

Black embroidery thread, small amount

GAUGE

Gauge is not critical for this project. Ensure your stitches are tight so the stuffing won't show through.

SPECIAL STITCHES

Invdec (invisible single crochet decrease): Insert hook in front loop only of each of next 2 sts, yarn over and draw through both sts, yarn over and draw through 2 loops on hook – 1 st decreased.

NOTES

Work in continuous rounds unless otherwise indicated.

BODY

With **A**.

Rnd 1: Ch 9, sc in 2nd ch from hook, sc 6, 3 sc in last, rotate to work on underside of ch, sc 7, 3 sc in last – 20 sc.

Rnd 2: *Sc 7, 2 sc in next 3 sts; rep from * around – 26 sc.

Rnd 3: *Sc 7, [2 sc, sc in next] x 3; rep from * around – 32 sc.

Rnd 4: *Sc 7, [2 sc, sc 2] x 3; rep from * around – 38 sc.

Rnd 5 (Tail Feathers): *Sc 11, [working in next st (ch 6, sc)] x 6, sc 21 – 38 sc, 6 ch-6 spaces.

Rnd 6: Sc 11, pushing ch-6 spaces forward to RS sc in next 6 sts, sc 21 – 38 sc.

Rnd 7: Sc around.

Rnd 8 (Tail Feathers): *Sc 11, [working in next st (ch 9, sc)] x 6, sc 21 – 38 sc, 6 ch-9 spaces.

Rnds 9–10: Rep Rnds 6–7.

Rnds 11–13: Rep Rnds 8–10.

Continue to Head.

HEAD

Rnd 1: Sc 6, skip next 20 sts, sc 12 – 18 sc.

Rnds 2–5: Sc around.

Rnd 6: [Invdec, sc] around – 12 sc.

Rnd 7: Invdec around – 6 sc.

Fasten off, leaving a long tail for sewing. Sew remaining 6 sts closed. Stuff Head and Body.

SEAMING

With **A** and starting at nape of neck, seam 7 sts on each side of Body together through both thicknesses (14 sts total, 7 for each side of seam), leaving 3 sts on either side of Tail unworked (6 Tail sts total). Continue to Tail.

TAIL

With **A**, join to any of 6 skipped sts of Tail left from seaming.

Rnds 1–3: Sc around – 6 sc.

Rnd 4: *Working in next st (ch 9, sc); rep from * around – 6 sc, 6 ch-9 spaces.

Fasten off, leaving a long tail for sewing. Sew remaining 6 sts closed. Weave in ends.

CREST

With **B** and leaving a long tail at start for sewing.

Rnd 1: Ch 6, sl st to form a ring, ch 3 (*counts as 1st dc*), 11 dc in ring, join – 12 dc.

Rnd 2: Ch 1, sc2tog around – 6 sc.

Fasten off, weave in finishing tail. Using starting tail, sew Crest to top of Head.

WINGS (MAKE 2)

With **A**.

Rnd 1: Ch 5, sc in 2nd ch from hook, sc 2, 3 sc in last, rotate to work on underside of starting ch, sc 3, 3 sc in last – 12 sc.

Fasten off, leaving a long tail for sewing. Sew to sides of Body.

BEAK

With **C**.

Row 1: Ch 3, sc in 2nd ch from hook, tr in last – 2 sts.

Fasten off, leaving a tail for sewing. Sew to front of Head.

FEET (MAKE 2)

With **C**.

Row 1: Ch 2, 3 sc in 2nd ch from hook, turn – 3 sc.

Row 2: Ch 1, 2 sc in each st across – 6 sc.

Fasten off, leaving a long tail for sewing. Sew Feet to bottom of Body.

FINISHING

Using black embroidery thread and with photo as a guide, add 2 short lines on either side of Head for eyes. Weave in ends.

GERALT

SKILL LEVEL: 

Featured in the *Witcher* franchise's many books, games, shows, and comics, Geralt of Rivia is quite the well-traveled witcher, going wherever his monster-slaying expertise is needed astride his trusty steed, Roach. While his cynical and gruff nature doesn't make for the best first impression, especially when combined with his reluctance to become involved in matters that don't concern him, he is a loyal and caring friend to those close to him. Oh, and he's not actually from Rivia.

FINISHED MEASUREMENTS

Height: 13.5 in. / 34.29 cm

Width: 8 in. / 20.32 cm

YARN

Worsted weight (#4 medium) yarn, shown in Lion Brand Yarn *Basic Stitch Anti Pilling* (100% acrylic, 185 yd. / 170 m per 3.5 oz. / 100 g skein).

Color A: #153 Black, 1 skein

Color B: #404J Silver Heather, 1 skein

Color D: #009T Ivory, 1 skein

Color E: #100 White, 1 skein

Worsted weight (#4 medium) yarn, shown in Lion Brand Yarn *Heartland* (100% acrylic, 251 yd. / 230 m per 5 oz. / 142 g skein).

Color C: #126 Sequoia, 1 skein

Worsted weight (#4 medium) yarn, shown in Furls Crochet *Wander* (100% acrylic, 120 yd. / 109 m per 3.5 oz. / 100 g skein).

Color F: Foundry, 1 skein

HOOK

US G/6 (4 mm) crochet hook

NOTIONS

Locking stitch markers

Tapestry needle

Polyester stuffing

Plastic mesh, small amount

Pair of 9 mm yellow safety eyes

Burgundy and red embroidery thread, small amounts

NOTES

Work in continuous rounds unless otherwise indicated.

ARMS (MAKE 2)

With **A**, make a magic ring.

Rnd 1: 6 sc in ring – 6 sc.

Rnd 2: 2 sc in each st around – 12 sc.

Rnds 3–4: Sc around.

Rnd 5: Popcorn, sc 11 – 12 sts.

Rnds 6–7: Sc around.

Rnd 8: Working in FLO, 2 sc in each st around, join to 1st sc with a sl st – 24 sc.

Rnd 9: Ch 1, in BLO of Rnd 8 sts sc around, join to 1st sc with a sl st – 12 sc.

Change to **B**.

Rnd 10: Ch 1, in BLO sc around, join – 12 sc.

Rnd 11: Ch 1, 2 sc in 1st st, sc around, join – 13 sc.

Rnd 12: Ch 1 tightly, sc around, *do not join* – 13 sc.

Rnd 13: 2 sc in 1st st, sc around – 14 sc.

Rnd 14: Sc around.

Change to **A**.

Rnd 15: Ch 1, working in BLO 2 sc in 1st st, sc around, join – 15 sc.

Rnds 16–18: Ch 1, sc around, join.

Fasten off. Stuff Arms and set aside to join to Body.

WRISTBANDS (MAKE 4)

With **C**.

Row 1: Ch 12.

Fasten off. Sew around each wrist, above and below Rnd 8 sts. Weave in ends.

BOOT SOLES (MAKE 4)

With **C**.

Rnd 1: Ch 5, sc in 2nd ch from hook, sc 2, 3 sc in last, rotate to work on underside of ch, sc 3, 3 sc in last – 12 sc.

Rnd 2: *Sc 3, [2 sc in next st] x 3; rep from * around – 18 sc.

Rnd 3: *Sc 3, [2 sc, sc in next] x 3; rep from * around – 24 sc.

Fasten off 1st piece, but do not fasten off 2nd piece. Trace Boot Sole on a piece of plastic mesh. Cut out the shape and place mesh between 2 Boot Soles and continue to joining rnd.

Rnd 4 (joining): Working in BLO through both thicknesses, with plastic mesh sandwiched in between, sc around – 24 sc.

Fasten off. Continue to Boots.

BOOTS (MAKE 2)

With **C**, join to back of heel of Boot Sole.

Rnds 1–2: Ch 1, sc around, join – 24 sc.

Rnd 3: Ch 1, sc 8, [invdec, sc] x 3, sc 7, join – 21 sc.

Rnd 4: Ch 1, sc 8, [invdec] x 3, sc 7, join – 18 sc.

Rnds 5–8: Sc around.

Fasten off.

LEGS (MAKE 2)

With **A**, join to center back of heel.

Rnd 1: Ch 1, in BLO sc around, join – 18 sc.

Rnd 2: Ch 1 tightly, sc around, *do not join* – 18 sc.

Rnds 3–12: Sc around.

Fasten off 1st Leg, but do not fasten off 2nd Leg.

Rnd 13 (joining): Sc around, sl st in same st as 1st sc (sl st not counted as a st), sc in middle of inner thigh of 2nd Leg, sc around – 36 sc.

Rnds 14–21: Sc around.

Continue to Body.

BODY

Continuing with **A**.

Rnd 1: Ch 1, working in FLO 2 sc in each st around, join – 72 sc.

Rnd 2: Ch 1, working in BLO sts left from Rnd 1, sc around, join – 36 sc.

Rnd 3: Ch 1 tightly, [2 sc, sc 11] x 3, *do not join* – 39 sc.

Rnd 4: [Sc 6, 2 sc, sc 6] around – 42 sc.

Rnd 5: [2 sc, sc 13] around – 45 sc.

Rnd 6: [Sc 7, 2 sc, sc 7] around – 48 sc.

Rnd 7: [2 sc, sc 15] around – 51 sc.

Rnd 8: [Sc 8, 2 sc, sc 8] around – 54 sc.

Using 2 locking stitch markers, mark sides of Body for Arms, ensuring there are 26 sts for front of Body and 26 sts for back of Body between markers.

Rnd 9: Sc to 1st marker, sc in marker, holding Arm join by sc 15 around Arm ensuring thumb is facing Body, sc to 2nd marked st, sc in marked st, holding 2nd Arm in line with Body and with thumb facing Body, sc 15 around Arm to join, sc in remaining sts around – 84 sc.

Rnds 10–12: Sc around.

Rnd 13: [Sc 6, invdec, sc 6] around – 78 sc.

Rnd 14: [Invdec, sc 11] around – 72 sc.

Rnd 15: [Sc 5, invdec, sc 5] around – 66 sc.

Rnd 16: [Invdec, sc 9] around – 60 sc.

Rnd 17: [Sc 4, invdec, sc 4] around – 54 sc.

Rnd 18: [Invdec, sc 7] around – 48 sc.

Rnd 19: [Sc 3, invdec, sc 3] around – 42 sc.

Rnd 20: [Invdec, sc 5] around – 36 sc.

Rnd 21: [Sc 2, invdec, sc 2] around – 30 sc.

Rnd 22: [Invdec, sc 3] around – 24 sc.

Rnd 23: [Sc, invdec, sc] around – 18 sc.

Rnds 24–26: Sc around.

Fasten off. Stuff Body firmly, paying attention to stuffing shoulders. Continue to Head.

HEAD

With **D**.

Rnd 1: [2 sc, sc] around – 36 sc.

Rnds 2–15: Sc around.

Add safety eyes between Rnds 10–11, approximately 6 sts apart. Using **D**, add nose over 3 sts between Rnds 8–9. Using **B**, add eyebrows over eyes. Using burgundy thread, embroider a scar over eyes using photo as a guide. Stuff Head and continue stuffing as work progresses.

Rnd 16: [Sc 2, invdec, sc 2] around – 30 sc.

Change to **E**.

Rnd 17: Ch 1, working in BLO, [invdec, sc 3] around – 24 sc.

Rnd 18: [Sc, invdec, sc] around – 18 sc.

Rnd 19: [Invdec, sc] around – 12 sc.

Rnd 20: Invdec around – 6 sc.

Fasten off, leaving a long tail for sewing. Sew remaining 6 sts closed. Weave in ends.

HAIR: LONG STRANDS (MAKE 8)

With **E**.

Row 1: Ch 31, sc in 2nd ch from hook and in each across – 30 sc.

Fasten off, leaving a long tail for sewing. Sew to top of Head, securing each as Long Strand reaches across to back of neck. Weave in ends.

HAIR: SHORT STRANDS (MAKE 4)

With **E**.

Row 1: Ch 7, sc in 2nd ch from hook, sc 6 – 6 sc.

Fasten off, leaving a long tail for sewing. Sew 1st 2 Short Strands to sides of Head in line with eyes. Sew 2nd Strands beneath 1st Strands on either side of Head. Weave in ends.

CROSSBODY STRAPS (MAKE 2)

With **C**.

Row 1: Ch 51, sc in 2nd ch from hook and in each across – 50 sc.

Fasten off, leaving a long tail for sewing. Sew ends together. Add Straps across from left shoulder to right hip, and from right shoulder to left hip, crossing in the middle of torso.

WAIST ARMOR

With **C**.

Row 1: Ch 4, sc in 2nd ch from hook and in each across, turn – 4 sc.

Rows 2–24: Ch 1, sc across, turn.

Change to **F**.

Rows 25–36: Ch 1, sc across, turn.

Fasten off. Sew Row 1 to Row 36. Using **C**, join to row ends.

Rnd 37: Ch 1, sc in each row end around, join – 36 sc.

Fasten off. Rep Rnd 37 for opposite edge.

Fasten off and secure around waist, with **F** facing the front.

SHOULDER ARMOR (MAKE 4)

With **F**.

Row 1: Ch 7, sc in 2nd ch from hook and in each across, turn – 6 sc.

Rows 2–7: Ch 1, sc across, turn.

Rnd 8: Ch 1, sc 6, *do not turn*, ch 1, rotate to work in row ends, sc 8, ch 1, sc 6 across underside of starting ch, ch 1, sc 8 in row ends, join – 28 sc.

Change to **C**.

Rnd 9: Ch 1, sc 6, ch 2, sc 8, ch 2, sc 6, ch 2, sc 6, ch 1, join – 28 sc.

Fasten off, leaving a long tail for sewing. Sew 1st 2 Armor pieces to Arm in line with end of gray patch. Sew 2nd 2 Armor pieces at neck, overlapping lower piece. Weave in ends.

ARM STRAPS (MAKE 2)

With **C**.

Row 1: Ch 20.

Fasten off, leaving a tail for sewing. Secure around lower Shoulder Armor on each Arm.

Weave in ends.

NECKLACE

With **B**.

Row 1: Ch 40.

Fasten off, leaving a tail for sewing. Secure around neck under Shoulder Armor. Weave in ends.

NECKLACE CHARM

With **F**, make a magic ring.

Rnd 1: (Sc, ch 2, sc, ch 4, sc 2, ch 4, sc, ch 2, sc) in ring, join – 6 sc.

Fasten off, leaving a tail for sewing. Using red embroidery thread, embroider small lines for eyes. Sew Charm to Necklace.

SANS

SKILL LEVEL: ★ ★ ★

A jokester and a pal, the skeleton Sans is there from the very beginning, watching Frisk as they traverse the many traps Sans's brother Papyrus has set up to capture them so King Asgore can take the monsters to the surface. While he is far less concerned about capturing the human child than Papyrus, he is a force to be reckoned with. Plenty of choices can be made over the course of *Undertale*—those walking a path of peace will receive quite the praise from Sans at the end of their journey, while those who were not *quite* pacifistic might get a harsh word or two. But for the merciless . . . they will find no mercy from Sans in return.

FINISHED MEASUREMENTS

Height: 12 in. / 30.48 cm

Width: 10 in. / 25.4 cm

YARN

Worsted weight (#4 medium) yarn, shown in Lion Brand Yarn *Basic Stitch Anti Pilling* (100% acrylic, 185 yd. / 170 m per 3.5 oz. / 100 g skein).

Color A: #100 White, 1 skein

Color B: #185S Peachy, 1 skein

Color C: #153 Black, 1 skein

Color D: #111R Royal Blue, 1 skein

Color E: #404J Silver Heather, 1 skein

HOOK

US G/6 (4 mm) crochet hook

NOTIONS

Locking stitch markers

Polyester stuffing

Plastic mesh, small amount

Tapestry needle

Black and white felt, small amount

Fabric glue

Black embroidery thread, small amount

GAUGE

Gauge is not critical for this project. Ensure your stitches are tight so the stuffing won't show through.

SPECIAL STITCHES

Invdec (invisible single crochet decrease): Insert hook in front loop only of each of next 2 sts, yarn over and draw through both sts, yarn over and draw through 2 loops on hook – 1 st decreased.

Popcorn (popcorn stitch): Work 5 dc in next st, drop loop on hook, insert hook from front to back in 1st dc of 5, place dropped loop on hook and draw it through the back of the 1st dc.

NOTES

Work in continuous rounds unless otherwise indicated.

ARMS (MAKE 2)

With **A**, make a magic ring.

Rnd 1: 6 sc in ring – 6 sc.

Rnd 2: 2 sc in each st around – 12 sc.

Rnds 3–4: Sc around.

Rnd 5: Popcorn, sc 11 – 12 sts.

Rnds 6–7: Sc around.

Rnd 8: In BLO, sc around – 12 sc.

Rnds 9–10: Sc around.

Rnd 11: Ch 1, 2 sc in 1st st, sc around, join – 13 sc.

Change to **C**.

Rnd 12: Ch 1 tightly, sc around, *do not join* – 13 sc.

Rnd 13: 2 sc in 1st st, sc around – 14 sc.

Rnd 14: Sc around.

Rnd 15: 2 sc in 1st st, sc around – 15 sc.

Rnds 16–18: Sc around.

Stuff Arms. Set aside to join to Body.

SLIPPER SOLES (MAKE 4)

With **B**.

Rnd 1: Ch 5, sc in 2nd ch from hook, sc 2, 3 sc in last, rotate to work on underside of ch, sc 3, 3 sc in last – 12 sc.

Rnd 2: *Sc 3, [2 sc in next st] x 3; rep from * around – 18 sc.

Rnd 3: *Sc 3, [2 sc, sc in next] x 3; rep from * around – 24 sc.

Fasten off 1st piece, but do not fasten off 2nd piece. Trace Slipper Sole on a piece of plastic mesh. Cut out the shape and place mesh between 2 Slipper Soles and continue to joining rnd.

Rnd 4 (joining): Working in BLO through both thicknesses, with plastic mesh sandwiched in between, sc around – 24 sc.

Fasten off. Continue to Feet.

FEET (MAKE 2)

With **A** and in BLO, join to back of heel of Slipper Sole.

Rnd 1: Ch 1, working in BLO sc around, join – 24 sc.

Rnd 2: Ch 1 tightly, sc around, join.

Rnd 3: Ch 1, sc 8, [invdec, sc] x 3, sc 7, join – 21 sc.

Rnd 4: Ch 1, sc 8, [invdec] x 3, sc 7, join – 18 sc.

Rnd 5: Ch 1, sc 6, [invdec] x 3, sc 6, join – 15 sc.

Rnd 6: Ch 1, sc 5, [invdec] x 3, sc 4, join – 12 sc.

Continue to Legs.

LEGS (MAKE 2)

Continuing with **A**.

Rnds 1–12: Sc around.

Fasten off.

SLIPPER TOPS (MAKE 2)

With **B**.

Row 1: Ch 2, 3 sc in 2nd ch from hook, turn – 3 sc.

Row 2: Ch 1, 2 sc across, turn – 6 sc.

Row 3: Ch 1, [2 sc, sc] across, turn – 9 sc.

Row 4: Ch 1, [2 sc, sc 2] across, turn – 12 sc.

Row 5: Ch 1, [2 sc, sc 3] across, *do not turn* – 15 sc.

Row 6: Ch 1, sc 11 evenly across row ends – 11 sc.

Fasten off, leaving a long tail for sewing. Sew to top of Foot. Weave in ends.

BODY

Using 2 locking stitch markers, mark inner thigh of each Leg where Legs will join. With **A** and left Leg, join to marked st.

Rnd 1: Sc around 1st Leg, ch 6, sc in marked st of right Leg – 24 sc.

Rnd 2: Sc in next 6 chs, sc 12, sc in underside of next 6 chs, sc 12 – 36 sc.

Rnd 3: Sc 12, [sc, 2 sc in next, sc] x 6, sc 6 – 42 sc.

Rnd 4: Sc 12, [2 sc, sc 3] x 6, sc 6 – 48 sc.

Rnds 5–9: Sc around.

Rnd 10: Working in BLO, sc around.

Rnds 11–16: Sc around.

Using 2 locking stitch markers, mark sides of Body for Arms, ensuring there are 23 sts for front of Body and 23 sts for back of Body between markers.

Rnd 17: Sc to 1st marker, sc in marker, holding Arm join by sc 15 around Arm ensuring thumb is facing Body, sc to 2nd marked st, sc in marked st, holding 2nd Arm in line with Body and with thumb facing Body, sc 15 around Arm to join, sc in remaining sts around – 78 sc.

Rnds 18–20: Sc around.

Rnd 21: [Invdec, sc 11] around – 72 sc.

Rnd 22: [Sc 5, invdec, sc 5] around – 66 sc.

Rnd 23: [Invdec, sc 9] around – 60 sc.

Rnd 24: [Sc 4, invdec, sc 4] around – 54 sc.

Rnd 25: [Invdec, sc 7] around – 48 sc.

Rnd 26: [Sc 3, invdec, sc 3] around – 42 sc.

Rnd 27: [Invdec, sc 5] around – 36 sc.

Rnd 28: [Sc 2, invdec, sc 2] around – 30 sc.

Rnd 29: [Invdec, sc 3] around – 24 sc.

Rnd 30: [Sc, invdec, sc 2] around – 18 sc.

Rnd 31: [Invdec, sc] around – 12 sc.

Stuff Body firmly, paying attention to stuffing shoulders. Continue to Neck.

NECK

Continuing with **A**.

Rnd 1: In BLO, sc around.

Rnd 2: Sc around.

Continue to Head.

HEAD

Continuing with **A**.

Rnd 1: 2 sc in each st around – 24 sc.

Rnd 2: [2 sc, sc] around – 36 sc.

Rnd 3: [Sc, 2 sc, sc] around – 48 sc.

Rnds 4–17: Sc around.

Using photo as a guide, cut out 2 pieces of black felt for the eyes and glue to Head between Rnds 11–13. Glue a small circle of white felt to each eye. Using black felt, cut a nose and glue between Rnds 8–11. Using black embroidery thread, embroider teeth 2 rnds below nose. Stuff Head and continue stuffing as work progresses.

Rnd 18: [Sc 3, invdec, sc 3] around – 42 sc.

Rnd 19: [Invdec, sc 5] around – 36 sc.

Rnd 20: [Sc 2, invdec, sc 2] around – 30 sc.

Rnd 21: [Invdec, sc 3] around – 24 sc.

Rnd 22: [Sc, invdec, sc] around – 18 sc.

Rnd 23: [Invdec, sc] around – 12 sc.

Rnd 24: Invdec around – 6 sc.

Fasten off, leaving a long tail for sewing. Sew remaining 6 sts closed. Weave in ends.

SHORTS (MAKE 2)

With **C**.

Rnd 1: Ch 18, sl st to form a ring, ch 1, sc 18 around, join – 18 sc.

Rnds 2–7: Ch 1, sc around, join.

Fasten off 1st piece, but do not fasten off 2nd piece.

Rnd 8 (joining): Ch 3, sc in 1st piece and in each sc around, 2 sc in each of the next 3 chs, sc around 2nd piece, 2 sc in each underside of the next 3 chs – 48 sc.

Rnds 9–11: Sc around.

Fasten off, leaving a long tail for sewing. Sew Shorts to FLO sts left from Rnd 10 of Body. Weave in ends.

JACKET SLEEVES (MAKE 2)

With **D**.

Row 1: Ch 4, sc in 2nd ch and in each across, turn – 3 sc.

Rows 2–18: Ch 1, in BLO sc across, turn – 3 sc.

Row 19: Ch 1, working through both thicknesses, sl st 3 through Row 18 and Row 1 to join.

Rnd 20: Rotate to work in row ends, ch 1, sc 18 evenly around, join – 18 sc.

Rnds 21–28: Ch 1, sc around, join – 18 sc.

Fasten off. Set Sleeves aside to join to Jacket.

JACKET

With **D**.

Row 1: Ch 4, sc in 2nd ch from hook, sc 2, turn – 3 sc.

Rows 2–48: Ch 1, working in BLO sc across, turn.

Row 49: Rotate to work in row ends, ch 1, sc 48 evenly across row ends, turn – 48 sc.

Rows 50–63: Ch 1, sc across, turn.

Row 64: Ch 1, sc 12, holding Sleeve in line with sts sc 15 around Sleeve, sc 24, holding 2nd Sleeve in line with sts sc 15 around 2nd Sleeve, sc 12, turn – 78 sc.

Row 65: Ch 1, [invdec, sc 11] across, turn – 72 sc.

Row 66: Ch 1, [invdec, sc 10] across, turn – 66 sc.

Row 67: Ch 1, [invdec, sc 9] across, turn – 60 sc.

Row 68: Ch 1, [invdec, sc 8] across, turn – 54 sc.

Row 69: Ch 1, [invdec, sc 7] across, turn – 48 sc.

Row 70: Ch 1, [invdec, sc 6] across, turn – 42 sc.

Row 71: Ch 1, [invdec, sc 5] across, turn – 36 sc.

Fasten off.

JACKET TRIM

With **D**, join to bottom right edge of Jacket.

Row 1: Ch 1, sc in each row end to neckline, sc across neckline, sc across opposite edge row ends, fasten off.

Change to **E**.

Row 2: Join to 1st st of Row 1, working in BLO sc across.

Fasten off and weave in ends.

HOOD

With **E**, leave a long tail at start for sewing.

Row 1: Ch 37, sc in 2nd ch from hook and in each across, turn – 36 sc.

Rows 2–22: Ch 1, sc across, turn.

Row 23: Fold piece in half, meeting 1st and last st of Row 22 together, ch 1, sc through both thicknesses over 18 sts.

Fasten off and weave in finishing end. Turn Hood inside out to place seam inside of Hood. Using starting tail, sew Hood around neckline of Jacket. Weave in ends.

FINISHING

With **E**, add braided drawstrings to either side of Hood. Place Jacket on Body.

HUGGY WUGGY

SKILL LEVEL: 

With long, warm arms and a happy smile, Huggy Wuggy's soft, gentle design was meant to give hugs to children in need. The appearance of Huggy Wuggy was later used to create a guardian for the Playtime Co. factory, though it harbored some dark secrets within it. Later, when The Prototype corrupted the toys of the factory, Huggy Wuggy's directives also became distorted, leading to the toy hunting down any intruders in the factory—even former employees.

FINISHED MEASUREMENTS

Height: 10 in. / 25.4 cm

Width: 4 in. / 10.16 cm

YARN

Worsted weight (#4 medium) yarn, shown in Lion Brand Yarn *Basic Stitch Anti Pilling* (100% acrylic, 185 yd. / 170 m per 3.5 oz. / 100 g skein).

Color A: #157X Lemonade, 1 skein

Color B: #111R Royal Blue, 1 skein

Worsted weight (#4 medium) yarn, shown in Lion Brand Yarn *DIYarn* (100% acrylic, 65 yd. / 60 m per 1.05 oz. / 30 g skein).

Color C: #205-113B Red, small amount

HOOK

US G/6 (4 mm) crochet hook

NOTIONS

Locking stitch markers

Tapestry needle

Polyester stuffing

White and black felt, small amounts

Pair of 16 mm black safety eyes

Fabric glue

GAUGE

Gauge is not critical for this project. Ensure your stitches are tight so the stuffing won't show through.

SPECIAL STITCHES

Invdec (invisible single crochet decrease): Insert hook in front loop only of each of next 2 sts, yarn over and draw through both sts, yarn over and draw through 2 loops on hook – 1 st decreased.

Popcorn (popcorn stitch): Work 5 dc in next st, drop loop on hook, insert hook from front to back in 1st dc of 5, place dropped loop on hook and draw it through the back of the 1st dc.

NOTES

Work in continuous rounds unless otherwise indicated.

RIGHT FOOT

With **A**.

Rnd 1: Ch 2, 6 sc in 2nd ch from hook – 6 sc.

Rnd 2: 2 sc in each st around – 12 sc.

Rnds 3–4: Sc around.

Rnd 5: Popcorn in next st, sc 11 – 12 sts.

Rnd 6: Sc 3, ch 3, skip 3 sc (*leg hole made*), sc 6 – 9 sc.

Rnd 7: Sc in each st and ch around – 12 sc.

Rnd 8: Invdec around – 6 sc.

Fasten off, leaving a long tail for sewing. Sew remaining 6 sts closed. Stuff piece lightly.

LEFT FOOT

With **A**.

Rnds 1–5: Rep Rnds 1–5 of Right Foot.

Rnd 6: Sc 8, ch 3, skip 3 sc (*leg hole made*), sc in last – 9 sc.

Rnds 7–8: Rep Rnds 7–8 of Right Foot.

Fasten off, leaving a long tail for sewing. Sew remaining 6 sts closed. Stuff piece lightly.

LEGS (MAKE 2)

With **B**.

Rnd 1: Join to 1st skipped sc of Rnd 6 of Foot, sc in each of the 3 skipped sc, sc in gap between sc and next ch, sc in underside of next 3 chs, sc in gap before starting sc – 8 sc.

Rnds 2–32: Sc around.

Fasten off. Stuff Legs.

BODY

With **B**. Using 2 locking stitch markers, mark inside middle st of each Leg (*at inner thigh of each Leg, Popcorn st of each Foot should be on the inside edge*). Join to 1st marked st.

Rnd 1: Sc 8, ch 3, sc in next marked st, sc in next 7 on opposite Leg – 16 sc.

Rnd 2: Sc in next 3 chs, sc 8, sc in underside of next 3 chs, sc 8 – 22 sc.

Rnd 3: Sc, 2 sc in next, sc 10, 2 sc in next, sc 9 – 24 sc.

Rnd 4: [2 sc, sc 3] around – 30 sc.

Rnds 5–7: Sc around.

Rnd 8: [Sc 4, invdec, sc 4] – 27 sc.

Rnd 9: [Invdec, sc 7] around – 24 sc.

Rnd 10: [Sc 3, invdec, sc 3] around – 21 sc.

Rnd 11: [Invdec, sc 5] around – 18 sc.

Rnd 12: [Sc 2, invdec, sc 2] around – 15 sc.

Rnd 13: [Invdec, sc 3] around – 12 sc.

Stuff Body. Continue to Head.

HEAD

Continuing with **B**.

Rnd 1: [2 sc, sc] around – 18 sc.

Rnd 2: [2 sc, sc 5] around – 21 sc.

Rnd 3: [Sc 3, 2 sc, sc 3] around – 24 sc.

Rnd 4: [2 sc, sc 7] around – 27 sc.

Rnd 5: [Sc 4, 2 sc, sc 4] around – 30 sc.

Rnd 6: [2 sc, sc 9] around – 33 sc.

Rnd 7: [Sc 5, 2 sc, sc 5] around – 36 sc.

Rnds 8–14: Sc around.

Add white felt to back of safety eyes. Add safety eyes between Rnds 8–11, approximately 3 sts apart.

Pinch Head in half in line with Feet and mark side edge with a stitch marker. Sc to marked st to begin next rnd.

Rnd 15: Yo and draw up a tall loop to create 1st dc, dc in next 2 sts, hdc 3, sc 6, hdc 3, dc 6, hdc 3, sc 6, hdc 3, dc 3, join to 1st st – 36 sts.

Fasten off, leaving a long tail for sewing. Stuff Head lightly. Seam 18 sts on either side of Head widthwise, matching 6 sc to 6 sc on opposite edge.

HANDS (MAKE 2)

With **A**.

Rnds 1–5: Rep Rnds 1–5 of Right Foot.

Rnds 6–7: Sc around.

Rnd 8: Invdec around – 6 sc.

Fasten off, leaving a long tail for sewing. Sew remaining 6 sts closed. Weave in ends.

ARMS (MAKE 2)

With **B**, join to any st of Hand.

Rnd 1: [2 sc, sc 2] around – 8 sc.

Rnds 2–32: Sc around, stuffing as working progresses.

Fasten off, leaving a long tail for sewing. Sew Arms to sides of Body.

LIPS

With **C**.

Row 1: Ch approximately 40 sts tightly.

Fasten off, leaving a long tail for sewing.

FINISHING

Using black felt, cut out mouth shape to fit beneath eyes. Using white felt, trim small pieces for teeth, and secure teeth to mouth using glue. Glue mouth beneath eyes. Sew Lips around mouth and weave in ends. Using a strand of **B**, tie a bow around neck.

Alt
Fn
Shift
Enter
Ctrl
Del
Home
End
Num
7
8
4
5
1
2
3
0
Del

SUB-ZERO

SKILL LEVEL: ★★★

A familiar face to fans of the *Mortal Kombat* franchise, Sub-Zero has made an appearance in every main game in the series, usually as a hero—but it's not always the same person donning the signature mask and blue garb. The name is a code name and a mantle taken on by three different people over the course of the games' timelines—Bi-Han, his younger brother Kuai Liang, and their unnamed grandfather, who was the original bearer of the code name "Sub-Zero."

FINISHED MEASUREMENTS

Height: 13 in. / 33.02 cm

Width: 10 in. / 25.4 cm

YARN

Worsted weight (#4 medium) yarn, shown in Lion Brand Yarn *Basic Stitch Anti Pilling* (100% acrylic, 185 yd. / 170 m per 3.5 oz. / 100 g skein).

Color A: #153 Black, 1 skein

Color B: #116H Beech, 1 skein

Color C: #111R Royal Blue, 1 skein

HOOK

US G/6 (4 mm) crochet hook

NOTIONS

Stitch markers

Plastic mesh, small amount

Tapestry needle

Polyester stuffing

Pair of 8 mm black safety eyes

Black and purple embroidery thread, small amounts

Black felt, small amount

GAUGE

Gauge is not critical for this project. Ensure your stitches are tight so the stuffing won't show through.

SPECIAL STITCHES

Invdec (invisible single crochet decrease): Insert hook in front loop only of each of next 2 sts, yarn over and draw through both sts, yarn over and draw through 2 loops on hook – 1 st decreased.

NOTES

Work in continuous rounds unless otherwise indicated.

BOOT SOLES (MAKE 4)

With **A**.

Rnd 1: Ch 5, sc in 2nd ch from hook, sc 2, 3 sc in last, rotate to work on underside of ch, sc 3, 3 sc in last – 12 sc.

Rnd 2: *Sc 3, [2 sc in next st] x 3; rep from * around – 18 sc.

Fasten off 1st piece, but do not fasten off 2nd piece. Trace Boot Sole on a piece of plastic mesh. Cut out the shape and place mesh between 2 Boot Soles and continue to joining rnd.

Rnd 3 (joining): Working in BLO, through both thicknesses, with plastic mesh sandwiched in between, sc around – 18 sc.

Rnds 4–5: Sc around.

Rnd 6: Sc 3, [invdec] x 3, sc 9 – 15 sc.

Rnd 7: Sc 3, [invdec] x 3, sc 6 – 12 sc.

Rnd 8: Sc around.

LEGS (MAKE 2)

Rnd 9: Sc 11, 2 sc in last – 13 sc.

Rnd 10: Sc 12, 2 sc in last – 14 sc.

Rnd 11: Sc 13, 2 sc in last – 15 sc.

Rnds 12–14: Sc around.

Rnd 15: [2 sc, sc 4] around – 18 sc.

Rnds 16–19: Sc around.

Remove row marker and mark center back of Leg as new start of rnd. Sc to marker.

Rnd 20: Sc 6, [2 sc, sc] x 3, sc 6 – 21 sc.

Rnds 21–26: Sc around.

Using 2 locking stitch markers, mark inner thigh of each Leg.

Rnd 27 (joining): Sc to 1st marker, sc in marked st and in each st around, sc in marked st of 2nd Leg to join, sc around – 42 sc.

Rnds 28–36: Sc around.

BODY

Rnd 37: [2 sc, sc 13] around – 45 sc.

Rnd 38: [Sc 7, 2 sc, sc 7] around – 48 sc.

Rnd 39: [2 sc, sc 15] around – 51 sc.

Rnd 40: [Sc 8, 2 sc, sc 8] around – 54 sc.

Rnd 41: [2 sc, sc 17] around – 57 sc.

Rnd 42: [Sc 9, 2 sc, sc 9] around – 60 sc.

Rnds 43–52: Sc around.

Rnd 53: [Sc 4, invdec, sc 4] around – 54 sc.

Rnd 54: [Invdec, sc 7] around – 48 sc.

Rnd 55: [Sc 3, invdec, sc 3] around – 42 sc.

Rnd 56: [Invdec, sc 5] around – 36 sc.

Rnd 57: [Sc 2, invdec, sc 2] around – 30 sc.

Rnd 58: [Invdec, sc 3] around – 24 sc.

Rnd 59: [Sc, invdec, sc] around – 18 sc.

Rnd 60: [Invdec, sc] around – 12 sc.

Rnds 61–63: Sc around.

Fasten off. Stuff Body firmly. Continue to Head.

HEAD

With **B**, join to back of neck on Body.

Rnd 1: 2 sc in each st around – 24 sc.

Rnd 2: [2 sc, sc 3] around – 30 sc.

Rnds 3–16: Sc around.

Add safety eyes between Rnds 11–12, approximately 6 sts apart. Using black embroidery thread, add eyebrows above eyes. Using purple embroidery thread, add scar to right eye. Stuff Head and continue stuffing as work progresses.

Rnd 17: [Invdec, sc 3] around – 24 sc.

Rnd 18: [Sc, invdec, sc] around – 18 sc.

Rnd 19: [Invdec, sc] around – 12 sc.

Rnd 20: Invdec around – 6 sc.

Fasten off, leaving a long tail for sewing. Sew remaining 6 sts closed. Weave in ends.

MASK

With **C**.

Row 1: Ch 2, 3 sc in 2nd ch from hook, turn – 3 sc.

Row 2: Ch 1, sc, 2 sc in next, sc, turn – 4 sc.

Row 3: Ch 1, 3 sc, sc across to last, 3 sc in last, turn – 8 sc.

Rows 4–8: Rep Row 3 – 24, sc at end of Row 8.

Fasten off, leaving a long tail for sewing. Place Mask on a piece of black felt and trace shape, leaving a visible black edge around Mask. Sew Mask to felt. Sew Mask to front of face, with bottom of Mask touching neckline. Weave in ends.

HOOD

With **A**.

Rnd 1: Ch 2, 6 sc in 2nd ch from hook – 6 sc.

Rnd 2: 2 sc in each st around – 12 sc.

Rnd 3: [2 sc, sc in next] around – 18 sc.

Rnd 4: [Sc, 2 sc in next, sc] around – 24 sc.

Rnd 5: [2 sc, sc 3] around – 30 sc.

Rnds 6–9: Sc around.

Row 10: Sc 15, turn, leaving remaining sts unworked – 15 sc.

Rows 11–17: Ch 1, sc 15, turn.

Row 18: Ch 1, [sc2tog, sc 3] across, turn – 12 sc.

Row 19: Ch 1, [sc2tog, sc 2] across, turn – 9 sc.

Fasten off, leaving a long tail for sewing. Add Hood to Head and sew edges with tail, ensuring that Hood touches side edges of Mask and bottom of Hood touches neck. Weave in ends.

ARMOR UNDERLAYER (MAKE 2)

With **A**.

Row 1: Ch 11, sc in 2nd ch from hook and in each across, turn – 10 sc.

Rows 2–55: Ch 1, sc across, turn.

Fasten off, leaving a long tail for sewing. Drape Armor across each shoulder, and using **A**, secure to each shoulder at neckline. Using **A**, sew a seam from hip up approximately 1.5 in. / 3.81 cm in length. Sew center seam approximately 1.5 in. / 3.81 cm up in length from bottom on front and back to join pieces. Weave in ends.

ARMOR OUTER LAYER (MAKE 4)

With **C**.

Row 1: Ch 5, sc in 2nd ch from hook and in each across, turn – 4 sc.

Rows 2–3: Ch 1, 2 sc in 2 sts, sc across to last, 2 sc in last, turn – 8 sc at Row 3.

Rows 4–12: Ch 1, sc across, turn – 8 sc.

Row 13: Ch 1, 2 sc, sc 3, turn leaving remaining sts unworked – 5 sc.

Row 14: Ch 1, sc 4, 2 sc, turn – 6 sc.

Rows 15–33: Ch 1, sc across, turn.

Fasten off. Join to 1st unworked st of Row 13.

Row 34: Ch 1, sc 3, 2 sc in last, turn – 5 sc.

Row 35: Ch 1, 2 sc, sc 4, turn – 6 sc.

Rows 36–54: Ch 1, sc across, turn.

Fasten off 1st piece, but do not fasten off 2nd piece. Continue to joining row.

Row 55 (joining): Holding 2 pieces together, sc through both thicknesses around entire shape evenly.

Fasten off, leaving a long tail for sewing. Taking 2 finished pieces, secure at shoulders by sewing shoulder seams together. Drape Armor over Body.

BELT

With **C**.

Row 1: Ch 200.

Fasten off. Secure Belt by wrapping it a number of times around center of Body tightly and tie a knot.

KNEEPADS (MAKE 2)

With **C**, make a magic ring.

Rnd 1: 6 sc in ring – 6 sc.

Rnd 2: 2 sc in each st around, sl st in next st, ch 10, skip 6 sts, sl st in next – 12 sc.

Fasten off and weave in ends. Slide a Kneepad over each Leg.

SHIN PADS (MAKE 2)

With **C**.

Row 1: Ch 4, sc in 2nd ch from hook and in each across, turn – 3 sc.

Rows 2–3: Ch 1, sc across, turn.

Row 4: Ch 1, rotate to sc 3 evenly across row ends, ch 1, sc 3 on underside of starting ch, ch 1, sc 3 across row ends, ch 1, sc 3 across Row 3, join – 12 sc.

Fasten off, leaving a long tail for sewing. Sew Shin Pad to each Leg under Kneepad. Weave in ends.

THUMBS (MAKE 2)

With **B**, make a magic ring.

Rnd 1: 4 sc in ring – 4 sc.

Rnd 2: Sc around – 4 sc.

Fasten off and set aside to join to Hands.

HANDS (MAKE 2)

With **B**.

Rnd 1: Ch 2, 6 sc in 2nd ch from hook – 6 sc.

Rnd 2: 2 sc in each st around – 12 sc.

Rnds 3–4: Sc around.

Rnd 5 (joining): Holding Thumb in line with sts, sc 4 on Thumb, sc 12 on Hand – 16 sc.

Rnds 6–7: Sc around.

Rnd 8: [Invdec, sc] around – 12 sc.

Fasten off and continue to Arm.

ARMS (MAKE 2)

With **C**.

Rnd 1: Ch 1, sc around, join – 12 sc.

Rnd 2: Ch 1 tightly, 2 sc, sc around, join – 13 sc.

Rnds 3–4: Rep Rnd 2 – 15, sc at end of Rnd 4.

Rnds 5–7: Sc around – 15 sc.

Change to **B**.

Rnd 8: Working in BLO, sc around.

Rnds 9–10: Sc around.

Rnd 11: [2 sc, sc 4] around – 18 sc.

LEFT ARM ONLY

Sc to st in line with Thumb, ch 1, turn.

Row 12: Sc 9, turn – 9 sc.

Row 13: Ch 1, sc 9, sc in 9 skipped sts – 18 sc.

Rnd 14: Sc around.

RIGHT ARM ONLY

Sc to st in line with Thumb, *do not turn.*

Row 12: Sc 9, turn – 9 sc.

Row 13: Ch 1, sc 9, turn – 9 sc.

Rnd 14: Ch 1, sc 9, sc in 9 skipped sts – 18 sc.

BOTH ARMS, CONTINUED

Rnd 15: Sc around.

Row 16: Sc 9, turn – 9 sc.

Row 17: Ch 1, sc 9, turn – 9 sc.

Rnd 18: Ch 1, sc 9, sc in 9 skipped sts – 18 sc.

Rnds/Rows 19–26: Rep Rnds/Rows 15–18.

Rnd 27: Sc around.

Fasten off, leaving a long tail for sewing. Stuff Arms firmly, stretching out the short rows so they are smooth. Sew Arms to tops of shoulders under Armor. Weave in ends.

ARMBANDS (MAKE 2)

With **C**.

Row 1: Ch 18, sl st to form a ring.

Fasten off and secure Armband to each upper Arm and weave in ends.

MR. SATURN

SKILL LEVEL: ★

A race that makes its home in the Saturn Valley, the Mr. Saturns are much-loved characters in both *EarthBound* and *Mother*, and an unofficial mascot to fans of the *Mother* trilogy. Their language, Saturnian, is represented in a childlike, almost handwritten font. As the creators of the Phase Distorter and the Absolutely Safe Capsule alongside Dr. Andonuts, these round, innocent life-forms are capable of great feats of engineering, despite their lack of hands—and yet they can't draw an accurate map of their valley home!

FINISHED MEASUREMENTS

Height: 4.5 in. / 11.43 cm

Width: 3.5 in. / 8.89 cm

YARN

Worsted weight (#4 medium) yarn, shown in Loops & Threads *Impeccable* (100% acrylic, 285 yd. / 260 m per 4.5 oz. / 127 g skein).

Color: #01010 Heather, 1 skein

HOOK

US G/6 (4 mm) crochet hook

NOTIONS

Stitch markers

Tapestry needle

Polyester stuffing

Black and red felt, small amounts

Hole punch

Fabric glue

Black embroidery thread, small amount

GAUGE

Gauge is not critical for this project. Ensure your stitches are tight so the stuffing won't show through.

SPECIAL STITCHES

Invdec (invisible single crochet decrease): Insert hook in front loop only of each of next 2 sts, yarn over and draw through both sts, yarn over and draw through 2 loops on hook – 1 st decreased.

NOTES

Work in continuous rounds unless otherwise indicated.

BODY

Rnd 1: Ch 2, 6 sc in 2nd ch from hook – 6 sc.

Rnd 2: 2 sc in each st around – 12 sc.

Rnd 3: [2 sc, sc in next] around – 18 sc.

Rnd 4: [Sc, 2 sc in next, sc] around – 24 sc.

Rnd 5: [2 sc, sc 3] around – 30 sc.

Rnd 6: [Sc 2, 2 sc in next, sc 2] around – 36 sc.

Rnd 7: [2 sc, sc 5] around – 42 sc.

Rnds 8–13: Sc around.

Rnd 14: Ch 12, skip 12 sts, sc around – 30 sc.

Rnd 15: Sc in each ch and sc around – 42 sc.

Rnds 16–20: Sc around.

Rnd 21: [Invdec, sc 5] around – 36 sc.

Rnd 22: [Sc 2, invdec, sc 2] around – 30 sc.

Rnd 23: [Invdec, sc 3] around – 24 sc.

Rnd 24: [Sc, invdec, sc] around – 18 sc.

Rnd 25: [Invdec, sc] around – 12 sc.

Rnd 26: Invdec around – 6 sc.

Fasten off, leaving a long tail for sewing. Sew remaining 6 sts closed. Weave in ends.

NOSE

Fasten on to 1st skipped st of Rnd 14 of Body.

Rnd 1: Sc in next 12 sc, rotate to sc in underside of each ch in ch-12, join – 24 sc.

Rnd 2: [2 sc, sc 3] around – 30 sc.

Rnds 3–5: Sc around.

Rnd 6: [Invdec, sc 3] around – 24 sc.

Rnd 7: [Sc, invdec, sc] around – 18 sc.

Rnd 8: [Invdec, sc] around – 12 sc.

Rnd 9: Invdec around – 6 sc.

Fasten off, leaving a long tail for sewing. Sew remaining 6 sts closed. Weave in ends.

BOTTOM

Rnd 1: Ch 2, 6 sc in 2nd ch from hook – 6 sc.

Rnd 2: 2 sc in each st around – 12 sc.

Rnd 3: [2 sc, sc in next] around – 18 sc.

Rnd 4: [Sc, 2 sc in next, sc] around – 24 sc.

Rnd 5: [2 sc, sc 3] around – 30 sc.

Rnd 6: [Sc 2, 2 sc in next, sc 2] around – 36 sc.

Fasten off, leaving a long tail for sewing. Stuff Nose and Body. Sew Bottom to 36 sts of Body, stuffing as work progresses. Do not overstuff, as Bottom should remain flat. Weave in ends.

FEET (MAKE 2)

Rnd 1: Ch 2, 6 sc in 2nd ch from hook – 6 sc.

Rnd 2: 2 sc in each st around – 12 sc.

Rnds 3–7: Sc around.

Rnd 8: Invdec around – 6 sc.

Fasten off, leaving a long tail for sewing. Sew remaining 6 sts closed. Use tail to sew Feet to Bottom of Body.

FINISHING

Using black felt and a hole punch, punch out 2 circles for the eyes and glue between Rnds 10–11 of Body, with 6 sc between eyes. Using black felt, cut eyebrow shapes and glue above eyes. Using black embroidery thread, add whiskers and a strand of hair atop head. Using red felt, cut bow shape and glue to strand of hair.

ZOMBIE

SKILL LEVEL: ★★★

In the world of *Plants vs. Zombies*, a zombie apocalypse has struck, and everything must be used creatively to survive—including weaponizing a garden to repel the zombies hungry for brains! However, the zombies have taken the idea of resourcefulness to heart as well. These adaptable undead utilize whatever they can get their hands on—from a bucket for a helmet to a vaulting pole to pass the Wall-nuts blocking their way, with some even going so far as to try and freeze the garden with a Zamboni in their hunt for delicious brains.

FINISHED MEASUREMENTS

Height: 11.5 in. / 29.21 cm

Width: 8 in. / 20.32 cm

YARN

Worsted weight (#4 medium) yarn, shown in Furls Crochet *Wander* (100% acrylic, 120 yd. / 109 m per 3.5 oz. / 100 g skein).

Color A: Patina, 1 skein

Color G: Garnet, 1 skein

Worsted weight (#4 medium) yarn, shown in Lion Brand Yarn *Basic Stitch Anti Pilling* (100% acrylic, 185 yd. / 170 m per 3.5 oz. / 100 g skein).

Color B: #100 White, 1 skein

Color C: #134U Honey, 1 skein

Color D: #126 Mahogany, 1 skein

Color E: #111R Royal Blue, 1 skein

Color F: #153 Black, small amount

HOOK

US G/6 (4 mm) crochet hook

NOTIONS

Locking stitch markers

Plastic mesh, small amount

Tapestry needle

Polyester stuffing

Two bamboo rods

White and black embroidery thread, small amounts

SPECIAL STITCHES

Invdec (invisible single crochet decrease): Insert hook in front loop only of each of next 2 sts, yarn over and draw through both sts, yarn over and draw through 2 loops on hook – 1 st decreased.

Popcorn (popcorn stitch): Work 5 dc in next st, drop loop on hook, insert hook from front to back in 1st dc of 5, place dropped loop on hook and draw it through the back of the 1st dc.

NOTES

Work in continuous rounds unless otherwise indicated.

ARMS (MAKE 2)

With **A**, make a magic ring.

Rnd 1: 6 sc in ring – 6 sc.

Rnd 2: 2 sc in each st around – 12 sc.

Rnds 3–4: Sc around.

Rnd 5: Popcorn, sc 11 – 12 sts.

Rnds 6–7: Sc around.

Change to **B**.

Rnd 8: Ch 1, invdec around, join – 6 sc.

Rnd 9: Ch 1 tightly, sc around, *do not join* – 6 sc.

Rnds 10–18: Sc around.

Fasten off and set aside to join to Body.

SOLES (MAKE 4)

Make 2 with **C** and 2 with **D**.

Rnd 1: Ch 5, sc in 2nd ch from hook, sc 2, 3 sc in last, rotate to work on underside of ch, sc 3, 3 sc in last – 12 sc.

Rnd 2: *Sc 3, [2 sc in next] x 3; rep from * around – 18 sc.

Rnd 3: *Sc 3, [2 sc, sc in next] x 3; rep from * around – 24 sc.

Fasten off 1st piece, but do not fasten off 2nd piece. Trace

Sole on a piece of plastic mesh. Cut shape out and place mesh between 2 Soles (1 in each color) and continue to joining rnd.

Rnd 4 (joining): With **D**, working in BLO through both thicknesses, with plastic mesh sandwiched in between, sc around – 24 sc.

Fasten off. Continue to Boots.

BOOTS (MAKE 2)

With **D**, join to back of heel of Sole.

Rnd 1: Ch 1, sc 8, [sc, invdec] x 3, sc 7, join – 21 sc.

Rnd 2: Ch 1, sc 8, [invdec] x 3, sc 7, join – 18 sc.

Rnd 3: Ch 1, sc 6, [invdec] x 3, sc 6, join – 15 sc.

Rnd 4: Ch 1, sc 5, [invdec] x 3, sc 4, join – 12 sc.

Stuff heel lightly, but do not stuff toe area.

Rnd 5: Ch 1, working in BLO sc2tog around, join – 6 sc.

Fasten off and continue to Legs.

LEGS (MAKE 2)

With **A**, join to back of heel of Boot.

Rnd 1: Ch 1, sc around, join – 6 sc.

Rnd 2: Ch 1 tightly, sc around, *do not join* – 6 sc.

Rnds 3–14: Sc around.

Rnd 15: 2 sc around – 12 sc.

Rnd 16: [2 sc, sc] around – 18 sc.

Fasten off. Set aside to join to Pants.

RIGHT PANT LEG

With **E**.

Rnd 1: Ch 18, sl st to form a ring, ch 1, sc around, join – 18 sc.

Rnd 2: Ch 1 tightly, sc around, *do not join* – 18 sc.

Rnds 3–16: Sc around.

Fasten off. Weave in ends.

BOTTOM LEFT PANT LEG

With **E**.

Rnds 1–3: Rep Rnds 1–3 of Right Pant Leg. Do not weave in any ends, trim ends short. Insert piece on to bottom of Left Leg.

TOP LEFT PANT LEG

With **E**.

Rnd 1: Ch 36, join with a sl st to form a ring, ch 1, [sc in next ch, skip next ch] around, join – 18 sc.

Rnd 2: Ch 1 tightly, sc around, *do not join* – 18 sc.

Rnds 3–4: Sc around.

Do not fasten off. Continue to Pants.

PANTS

With **E**. This rnd will combine the tops of the Legs with the tops of the Pants by sc through both thicknesses.

Rnd 1: Starting in middle of inner thigh of Left Leg, sc around Top Left Pant Leg and Left Leg through both thicknesses to join them, holding Right Pant Leg and Right Leg together, sc in middle inner thigh of next Leg through both thicknesses, sc around, join – 36 sc.

Rnds 2–5: Sc around.

Rnd 6: [2 sc, sc 5] around – 42 sc.

Fasten off. Insert Bamboo Rod down each leg for structural support. Continue to Body.

BODY

With **B**, join to center back of Pants.

Rnd 1: In BLO, sc around – 42 sc.

Rnds 2–7: Sc around.

Using 2 locking stitch markers, mark sides of Body for Arms, ensuring there are 20 sts for front of Body and 20 sts for back of Body between markers.

Rnd 8: Sc to 1st marker, sc in marker, holding Arm join by sc 15 around Arm ensuring thumb is facing Body, sc to 2nd marked st, sc in marked st, holding 2nd Arm in line with Body and with thumb facing Body sc 15 around Arm to join, sc in remaining sts around – 54 sc.

Rnds 9–11: Sc around.

Rnd 12: [Invdec, sc 7] around – 48 sc.

Rnd 13: [Sc 3, invdec, sc 3] around – 42 sc.

Rnd 14: [Invdec, sc 5] around – 36 sc.

Rnd 15: [Sc 2, invdec, sc 2] around – 30 sc.

Rnd 16: [Invdec, sc 3] around – 24 sc.

Rnd 17: [Sc, invdec, sc] around – 18 sc.

Rnd 18: [Invdec, sc] around – 12 sc.

Fasten off. Stuff Body firmly, paying attention to stuffing shoulders. Continue to Head.

HEAD

With **A**.

Rnd 1: In BLO, 2 sc around, join – 24 sc.

Rnd 2: Ch 1 tightly, sc around, *do not join* – 24 sc.

Rnd 3: [2 sc, sc 7] around – 27 sc.

Using 2 locking stitch markers, mark center 6 sc in front of face for Mouth opening.

Rnd 4: Sc around to 1st marked st, ch 6, skip 6 marked sc (*Mouth opening made*), sc around in remaining sts – 21 sc.

Remove 2 Mouth markers.

Rnd 5: [Sc 4, 2 sc, sc 4] in each st and ch around – 30 sc.

Rnd 6: [2 sc, sc] x 6, sc 18 – 36 sc.

Rnd 7: [2 sc, sc 11] around – 39 sc.

Rnd 8: [Sc 6, 2 sc, sc 6] around – 42 sc.

Rnd 9: [2 sc, sc 13] around – 45 sc.

Rnd 10: [Sc 7, 2 sc, sc 7] around – 48 sc.

Rnds 11–13: Sc around.

Rnd 14: [Sc 3, invdec, sc 3] around – 42 sc.

Rnd 15: [Invdec, sc 5] around – 36 sc.

Rnd 16: [Sc 2, invdec, sc 2] around – 30 sc.

Rnd 17: [Invdec, sc 3] around – 24 sc.

Rnd 18: [Sc, invdec, sc] around – 18 sc.

Rnd 19: [Invdec, sc] around – 12 sc.

Rnd 20: Invdec around – 6 sc.

Fasten off, leaving a long tail for sewing. Sew remaining 6 sts closed. Weave in ends.

MOUTH

With **F**, make a magic ring.

Rnd 1: 6 sc in ring – 6 sc.

Rnd 2: 2 sc in each around – 12 sc.

Rnd 3: Sc around.

Fasten off, leaving a tail for sewing. Sew Mouth inside Mouth opening. Using **B**, embroider teeth at edges of Mouth. Weave in ends.

LARGE EYE

With **B**, make a magic ring.

Rnd 1: 6 sc in ring – 6 sc.

Rnd 2: 2 sc in each st around – 12 sc.

Rnd 3: Sc around.

Fasten off, leaving a long tail for sewing. Using black embroidery thread, embroider a small pupil onto Large Eye. Sew Large Eye to left side of face between Rnds 8–12. Weave in ends.

LARGE EYE TRIM

With **A**.

Row 1: Ch 12.

Fasten off, leaving a long tail for sewing. Sew around Large Eye. Weave in ends.

SMALL EYE

With **B**, make a magic ring.

Rnd 1: 6 sc in ring – 6 sc.

Rnd 2: Sc around.

Fasten off, leaving a long tail for sewing. Using black embroidery thread, embroider a small pupil onto Small Eye. Sew Small Eye to right side of face between Rnds 8–10. Weave in ends.

SMALL EYE TRIM

With **A**.

Row 1: Ch 6.

Fasten off, leaving a long tail for sewing. Sew around Small Eye. Weave in ends.

NECKTIE

With **G**, make a magic ring.

Rnd 1: 3 sc in ring – 3 sc.

Rnd 2: 2 sc, sc 2 – 4 sc.

Rnd 3: 2 sc around – 8 sc.

Rnd 4: [2 sc, sc 3] around – 10 sc.

Rnd 5: [2 sc, sc 4] around – 12 sc.

Rnd 6: Sc around.

Rnd 7: [Invdec, sc 4] around – 10 sc.

Rnds 8–15: Sc around.

Rnd 16: [2 sc, sc] around – 15 sc.

Rnd 17: [Invdec, sc 3] around – 12 sc.

Rnd 18: Invdec around – 6 sc.

Fasten off, leaving a long tail for sewing. Using white embroidery thread and photo as a guide, embroider slanted lines to front of Necktie. Sew Necktie to top of neck.

COLLAR (MAKE 2)

With **B**.

Row 1: Ch 2, 3 sc in 2nd ch from hook – 3 sc.

Fasten off, leaving a long tail for sewing. Sew Collars to front of neckline. Weave in ends.

JACKET SLEEVES (MAKE 2)

With **D**.

Rnd 1: Ch 15, sl st to form a ring, ch 1, sc in each ch around – 15 sc.

Rnd 2: Ch 1, sc around, join.

Rnd 3: Ch 1, working in FLO sl st around, join – 15 sl sts.

Rnd 4: Ch 1, working in BLO of Rnd 2, sc around, join – 15 sc.

Rnds 5–13: Sc around.

Fasten off. Set Jacket Sleeves aside to join to Jacket.

JACKET

With **D**.

Row 1: Ch 37, sc in 2nd ch from hook and in each across, turn – 36 sc.

Rows 2–8: Ch 1, sc across, turn.

Row 9: Ch 1, sc 9, holding Sleeve in line with sts sc 15 around Sleeve, sc 18, holding 2nd Sleeve in line with sts sc 15 around Sleeve, sc 8, turn – 66 sc.

Row 10: Ch 1, [sc2tog, sc 9] across, turn – 60 sc.

Row 11: Ch 1, [sc2tog, sc 8] across, turn – 54 sc.

Row 12: Ch 1, [sc2tog, sc 7] across, turn – 48 sc.

Row 13: Ch 1, [sc2tog, sc 6] across, turn – 42 sc.

Row 14: Ch 1, [sc2tog, sc 5] across, turn – 36 sc.

Row 15: Ch 1, [sc2tog, sc 4] across, turn – 30 sc.

Row 16: Ch 1, [sc2tog, sc 3] across, turn – 24 sc.

Row 17: Ch 1, [sc2tog, sc 2] across, turn – 18 sc.

Fasten off. Join to bottom right-hand corner of inside edge.

Rnd 18: Ch 1, sc 16 across row ends, sc 18 across back of neck, sc 16 across opposite edge row ends, sc 36 across underside of starting ch, join – 86 sc.

Fasten off. Skip 1st 4 sts from bottom right of Rnd 18 (4 sts from start of rnd). With **C**, join to next st.

Row 19: Ch 1, sc 12, turn – 12 sc.

Row 20: Ch 1, sl st in each st across – 12 sl st.

Fasten off. Weave in ends. Rep Rows 19–20 for opposite edge of Jacket.

MAMA

SKILL LEVEL: ⭐⭐

Mama, of *Cooking Mama* fame, is a passionate chef who is endlessly enthusiastic about passing on her knowledge. She has several dishes ranging from simple to complex that she's willing to teach players. While she might get a *little* upset when things go wrong, she's also extremely encouraging, congratulating each success and always allowing for another go after a dish ends in failure. Even if the dish gets burnt, don't worry—Mama will fix it!

FINISHED MEASUREMENTS

Height: 9 in. / 22.86 cm

Width: 5 in. / 12.7 cm

YARN

Worsted weight (#4 medium) yarn, shown in Lion Brand Yarn *Basic Stitch Anti Pilling* (100% acrylic, 185 yd. / 170 m per 3.5 oz. / 100 g skein), 1 skein each:

Color A: #100 White

Color B: #111R Royal Blue

Color D: #158I Mustard

Color E: #126 Mahogany

Worsted weight (#4 medium) yarn, shown in Loops & Threads *Impeccable* (100% acrylic, 285 yd. / 260 m per 4.5 oz. / 127 g skein).

Color C: #67 Heather, 1 skein

Worsted weight (#4 medium) yarn, shown in Furls Crochet *Wander* (100% acrylic, 120 yd. / 109 m per 3.5 oz. / 100 g skein).

Color F: Dahling

HOOK

US G/6 (4 mm) crochet hook

NOTIONS

Stitch markers

Tapestry needle

Polyester stuffing

Pair of 12 mm black safety eyes

Black embroidery thread, small amount

SPECIAL STITCHES

Invdec (invisible single crochet decrease): Insert hook in front loop only of each of next 2 sts, yarn over and draw through both sts, yarn over and draw through 2 loops on hook – 1 st decreased.

Popcorn (popcorn stitch): Work 5 dc in next st, drop loop on hook, insert hook from front to back in 1st dc of 5, place dropped loop on hook and draw it through the back of the 1st dc.

NOTES

Work in continuous rounds unless otherwise indicated.

SHOES (MAKE 2)

With **A**, make a magic ring.

Rnd 1: 6 sc in ring – 6 sc.

Rnd 2: 2 sc in each st around – 12 sc.

Rnd 3: Sc around.

Rnd 4: Ch 6, skip 6 sc, sc in remaining 6 sts – 6 sc.

Rnd 5: Sc in each ch and sc around – 12 sc.

Rnd 6: Invdec around – 6 sc.

Fasten off. Join with **A** to 1st skipped st of Rnd 4.

Rnd 7 (Ankle): Sc in each of the 6 skipped sts of Rnd 4, sc in gap before ch-6, sc 6 in underside of ch-6, sc in gap before 1st sc of rnd – 14 sc.

Fasten off and weave in ends. Continue to Legs.

LEGS (MAKE 2)

With **B**, join to back of Shoe.

Rnd 1: Sc around – 14 sc.

Rnd 2: [Invdec, sc 5] around – 12 sc.

Rnds 3–13: Sc around.

Fasten off 1st Leg, but do not fasten off 2nd Leg. Stuff each Leg. Continue to Body.

BODY

Continuing with **B**. Using 2 locking stitch markers, mark center of inner thigh of each Leg where Legs will join.

Rnd 1: Sc to 1st marked st, sc in marked st, sc in marked st of opposite Leg, sc around opposite Leg, sc in remaining sts – 24 sc.

Rnd 2: [2 sc, sc 3] around – 30 sc.

Rnds 3–5: Sc around.

Change to **A**.

Rnd 6: Working in BLO, sc around – 30 sc.

Rnds 7–14: Sc around.

Rnd 15: [Invdec, sc 3] around – 24 sc.

Rnd 16: [Sc, invdec, sc] around – 18 sc.

Rnd 17: [Invdec, sc] around – 12 sc.

Fasten off. Stuff Body. Continue to Head.

HEAD

With **C**, join to FLO of back of Body.

Rnd 1: Working in FLO, [2 sc, sc] around – 18 sc.

Rnd 2: [Sc, 2 sc in next, sc] around – 24 sc.

Rnd 3: [2 sc, sc 3] around – 30 sc.

Rnd 4: [Sc 2, 2 sc, sc 2] around – 36 sc.

Rnd 5: [2 sc, sc 5] around – 42 sc.

Rnds 6–15: Sc around.

Rnd 16: [Invdec, sc 5] around – 36 sc.

Add eyes between Rnds 10–11, approximately 6 sts apart. Using black thread, add eye details above and below eyes using photo as a guide. Using black thread, add mouth between Rnds 7–8. Stuff Head and continue stuffing as work progresses.

Rnd 17: [Sc 2, invdec, sc 2] around – 30 sc.

Rnd 18: [Invdec, sc 3] around – 24 sc.

Rnd 19: [Sc, invdec, sc] around – 18 sc.

Rnd 20: [Invdec, sc] around – 12 sc.

Rnd 21: Invdec around – 6 sc.

Fasten off, leaving a long tail for sewing. Sew remaining 6 sts closed. Weave in ends.

HANDS (MAKE 2)

With **C**.

Rnd 1: Ch 2, 6 sc in 2nd ch from hook – 6 sc.

Rnd 2: 2 sc in each st around – 12 sc.

Rnds 3–4: Sc around.

Rnd 5: Popcorn in 1st st, sc 11 – 12 sts.

Rnd 6: Sc around.

Rnd 7: Invdec around – 6 sc.

Fasten off and weave in ends. Stuff Hands lightly. Continue to Arms.

ARMS (MAKE 2)

With **A**.

Rnd 1: Sc around Hand – 6 sc.

Rnds 2–8: Sc around.

Fasten off, leaving a long tail for sewing. Sew to neckline on either side of Body. Weave in ends.

COLLAR (MAKE 2)

With **A**, make a magic ring.

Rnd 1: 3 sc in ring, pull ring closed tightly, ch 1 to fasten off – 3 sc.

Leave a long tail for sewing. Sew each piece of Collar directly under chin at top of shirt. Weave in ends.

APRON

With **D**.

Row 1: Ch 15, sc in 2nd ch from hook and in each st across, turn – 14 sc.

Rows 2–16: Ch 1, sc across, turn.

Row 17: Ch 1, sc in 1st st, sc2tog, sc across to last 3 sts, sc2tog, sc in last, turn – 12 sc.

Rows 18–20: Ch 1, sc across, turn – 12 sc.

Row 21: Ch 1, sc across, *do not turn* – 12 sc.

Row 22 (Border): Ch 1, rotate to work across row ends, sc 21 evenly across row ends, ch 1, sc 14 across bottom, ch 1, rotate to work on opposite edge and sc 21 evenly across row ends (*begin working Straps*) ch 15, sc in 2nd ch from hook and in each ch across, sc in 12 sts across top of Apron, ch 15, sc in 2nd ch from hook and in each ch across, join to 1st sc – 96 sc.

Fasten off and weave in ends. Tie Apron around neck using Straps. Using a length of **D** held double, tie a bow around the waist of the Apron.

HAIR

With **E**.

Rnd 1: Ch 2, 6 sc in 2nd ch from hook – 6 sc.

Rnd 2: 2 sc in each st around – 12 sc.

Rnd 3: [2 sc, sc in next] around – 18 sc.

Rnd 4: [Sc, 2 sc in next, sc] around – 24 sc.

Rnd 5: [2 sc, sc 3] around – 30 sc.

Rnd 6: [Sc 2, 2 sc in next, sc 2] around – 36 sc.

Rnd 7: [2 sc, sc 5] around – 42 sc.

Rnd 8: Sc around.

Rnd 9 (Hair Strands): [Ch 9, sc in 2nd ch from hook, sc in next 7 ch, sl st in next 2 sts of Rnd 8] x 15, [ch 7, sc in 2nd ch from hook, sc in next 5 chs, sl st in next 2 sts of Rnd 8] x 4, ch 5, sc in 2nd ch from hook, sc in next 3 chs, sl st in next 2 sts of Rnd 8 – 20 Strands of Hair worked.

Fasten off, leaving a long tail for sewing. Sew Hair to top of Head, with last Strand of Hair made resting above the right eye. Using a length of **F**, secure half of each side of Hair in a pigtail and flare the ends outward using photo as a guide. Weave in ends.

HEAD SCARF

With **F**.

Row 1: Ch 26, sc in 2nd ch from hook and in each ch across, turn – 25 sc.

Rows 2–8: Ch 1, sc across, turn – 25 sc.

Fasten off, leaving a long tail for sewing. Secure each side of Head Scarf to sides of Head using photo as a guide. Weave in ends.

EARS (MAKE 2)

With **C**, make a magic ring.

Rnd 1: 3 sc in ring, pull ring closed tightly, ch 1 to fasten off – 3 sc.

Leave a long tail for sewing. Sew each Ear to side of Head using photo as a guide. Weave in ends.

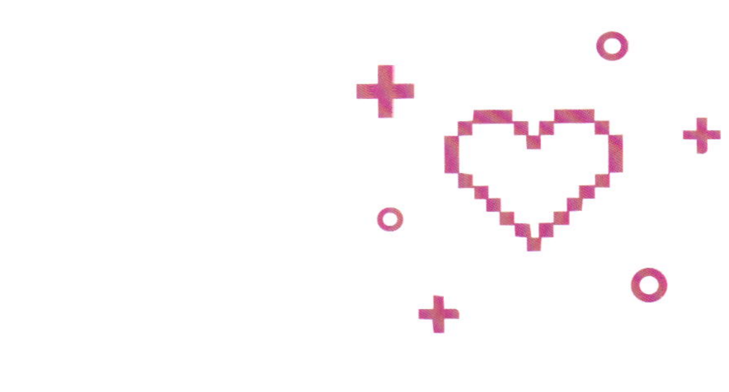

ABBREVIATIONS

BLO: back loop only
ch(s): chains
dc: double crochet
FLO: front loop only
fpsc: front post single crochet
hdc: half double crochet
invdec: invisible decrease
rep: repeat
rnd: round
sc: single crochet
sc2tog: single crochet 2 stitches together
sl st: slip stitch
st(s): stitch(es)
tr: treble crochet
yo: yarn over

YARN RESOURCE GUIDE

Furls Crochet Yarn: www.furlscrochet.com
Lion Brand Yarn: www.lionbrand.com
Loops & Threads Yarn: www.michaels.com
WeCrochet Yarn: www.crochet.com

PO Box 3088
San Rafael, CA 94912
www.insighteditions.com

Find us on Facebook: www.facebook.com/InsightEditions
Follow us on Instagram: @insighteditions

Published by Insight Editions, San Rafael, California, in 2026.

ISBN: 979-8-88663-688-8

Publisher: Raoul Goff
SVP, Group Publisher: Vanessa Lopez
VP, Creative: Chrissy Kwasnik
VP, Manufacturing: Alix Nicholaeff
Publishing Director: Mike Degler
Art Director: Catherine San Juan
Junior Designer: Samuel Louie
Executive Editor: Jennifer Sims
Senior Editor: Eric Geron
Editor: Sadie Lowry
Editorial Assistant: Jeff Chiarelli
Managing Editor: Nora Milman
Production Associate: Tiffani Patterson
Strategic Production Planner: Lina s Palma-Temena

Technical Editor: BJ Berti
Photographer: Stacy Ventura
Text by Lee Sartori and Kay Austin
Special thanks to Gavin Motnyk for his design support.

Insight Editions, in association with Roots of Peace, will plant two trees for each tree used in the manufacturing of this book. Roots of Peace is an internationally renowned humanitarian organization dedicated to eradicating land mines worldwide and converting war-torn lands into productive farms and wildlife habitats. Roots of Peace will plant two million fruit and nut trees in Afghanistan and provide farmers there with the skills and support necessary for sustainable land use.

Manufactured in China by Insight Editions
10 9 8 7 6 5 4 3 2 1